Praise for *People Buy You*

"*People Buy You* is not just a self-evident truth, it's your opportunity to discover why and how. Jeb Blount has written an easy-to-understand and easy-to-apply set of principles and actions that can help you earn more the minute you read them."

—Jeffrey Gitomer, author of *Little Red Book of Selling*

"Jeb Blount has written a practical, powerful book that will help any sales professional make more sales than ever before."

—Brian Tracy, author of *The Psychology of Selling*

"Jeb Blount nails it in *People Buy You*. When you turn yourself into the competitive differentiator, you're unstoppable."

—Jill Konrath, best-selling author of *SNAP Selling to Big Companies*

"Becoming a business leader or a sales champion transcends your ability to memorize a sales script or follow a regimented system. The real secret to unprecedented success starts with adopting this predominant universal law: Who you are is always more important than what you do. In *People Buy You*, Jeb Blount has effectively encapsulated this critical level of thinking. He delivers practical strategies to drive more sales and get more of what matters most in your life and career by leveraging your ultimate, authentic competitive edge—YOU!"

—Keith Rosen, executive sales coach and author of *Coaching Salespeople into Sales Champions*

"*People Buy You* is groundbreaking because it goes counter to all the other sales books being currently written that ignore common sense: that people matter most."

—Bob Beaudine, author of the best-selling *The Power of WHO*

"*People Buy You* should be required reading for any professional who wants to sell more, sell faster, and build a powerful brand that people talk about and refer others to. Jeb Blount breaks all sales myths, while exploring the right way to grow relationships, influence, and persuasion in the new economy."

—Dan Schawbel, best-selling author of *Me 2.0: Build a Powerful Brand to Achieve Career Success*

PEOPLE

THE REAL SECRET TO WHAT

BUY

MATTERS MOST IN BUSINESS

YOU

JEB BLOUNT

WILEY

John Wiley & Sons, Inc.

Published by John Wiley & Sons, Inc., Hoboken, New Jersey.
Published simultaneously in Canada.

For general information on our other products and services or for technical support, please contact our Customer Care Department within the United States at (800) 762-2974, outside the United States at (317) 572-3993 or fax (317) 572-4002.

Wiley also publishes its books in a variety of electronic formats. Some content that appears in print may not be available in electronic books. For more information about Wiley products, visit our web site at www.wiley.com.

Library of Congress Cataloging-in-Publication Data:

Blount, Jeb.
  People buy you : the real secret to what matters most in business / Jeb Blount.
    p. cm.
  ISBN 978-0-470-59911-2 (cloth); ISBN 978-0-470-64662-5 (ebk);
  ISBN 978-0-470-64681-6 (ebk); ISBN 978-0-470-64682-3 (ebk)
  1. Customer relations.   2. Interpersonal relations.   3. Selling.   I. Title.
  HF5415.5.B569 2010
  658.8–dc22

                                                            2010004444

Printed in the United States of America.

10 9 8 7 6 5 4 3

To Jebby

Contents

Foreword

As CEO of one of the major international executive recruiting firms, I get a chance every day to meet and interview the best talent in the country. It's what makes my job so much fun: meeting people with great leadership skills, unbelievable interpersonal skills, and vision. I'll never forget trying to recruit Jeb Blount many years back for a top position. He was highly recommended as one of the top relationship sales executives in his industry, and those recommendations were right. There was something that differentiated him—it was his people skills. Yes, that was it! He liked people and it showed! Well, I didn't get very far with Jeb; he loved where he was and the team he worked with. But our lunch turned out better—we became friends. Our friendship grew over the years, and turned into an opportunity for me to encourage Jeb with his other gifts and talents: speaking and writing. Now, here he is, about to knock the ball out of the park.

Jeb's new book, *People Buy You,* is groundbreaking because it goes counter to all the other sales books currently being written, which ignore common sense. They ignore the fact that people matter most. I found the same to be true in my experiences. I get 52,000 resumes a year sent to Dear Sir, To Whom It May Concern, and Dear Recruiter. What are they thinking? Dear Recruiter? That's an oxymoron isn't it? Well, just as we aren't born with all the skills we need, neither are we born with a strategy for living. *People Buy You* delivers a step-by-step strategy to help remind you that Grandma and Grandpa were right: Getting your clients to like you and trust you, having a good reputation— that's *gold!*

In my first sales job, I sold a wide assortment of canned products to the food services of schools and hospitals, and to restaurants. Each day, I had to cook up some product and put it in a thermos for my buyers to sample. Mrs. Perkins, who could've played the part of Aunt Bea of Mayberry, was the buyer at a school district in Lubbock, Texas. I arrived at 6:15 A.M. carrying a large product bag, fully looking the part of the dorky salesman. I was 22 years old and so intensely focused on selling what I had in my bag that it never dawned on me that Mrs. Perkins might not actually enjoy chili for breakfast with her morning coffee. When she saw me begin to unscrew the lid, kind Mrs. Perkins said, "Son, please don't open that thermos. It's 6:15 in the morning!" As I fumbled around in my bag to find a promo shot of the product, she began to ask me about my family. I found myself feeling very much at ease in her presence. For the next 45 minutes, Mrs. Perkins talked about her family, especially her grandchildren. I was getting a lesson in patience when it came to sales. She was so nice to me that day that I began to look forward to our next visit, hoping, of course, that somewhere along the line she'd buy some of my product. I closed my bag, prepared to leave, and, after a few more cordial remarks, I thanked her for taking the time to meet with me. As I headed toward the door I heard her say, "Bob, aren't you forgetting something?" I turned around, looking for whatever I had left behind. She said, "I'll take one hundred cases of chili." Overwhelmed, I ran over and hugged her! It was my first sale, and I learned a lesson that has stayed with me my whole life. It wasn't my pitch, my product, or even my company that landed my first big sale. It was my willingness to listen.

Are you looking for a competitive sales edge this year? Well, you're not going to find it in the *what* in life: the stuff, the brochures, resumes, PowerPoints, DVDs, or faceless web sites. No. But Jeb Blount has researched far and wide and provides irresistibly practical advice. If you're looking for a job, a better job, or you want to smash a sales record, stop here. Take some time to read *People Buy You*. Grandma and Grandpa would be proud. Trust me, I do this for a living!

Bob Beaudine, author, *The Power of WHO,*
and CEO of Eastman & Beaudine

About the Author

Jeb Blount is the CEO of SalesGravy.com, the most visited sales web site on the Internet. He is a respected thought leader, keynote speaker, and consultant who has helped companies, from Fortune 1000s to start-ups, develop winning sales, leadership, and client relationship strategies. He is the author of *Sales Guy's 7 Rules for Outselling the Recession* and *Power Principles*. His podcasts, *Power Principles* and *Sales Guy's Quick and Dirty Tips*, have been downloaded in excess of 4 million times, making him the most downloaded sales expert in iTunes history. More than 100,000 sales professionals and sales leaders subscribe to his weekly Sales Gravy eMagazine and he has written and published more than 100 articles on sales and leadership.

When it comes to sales and business relationships, Jeb has *"been there, done that, and has the t-shirts to prove it."* He has lived in trenches his entire career. As a sales rep, sales manager, director of sales, and vice president of sales he won virtually every sales award available at ARAMARK, the Fortune 500 company where he spent much of his career prior to founding Sales-Gravy.com. He was recognized as Account Executive of the Year, Sales Manager of the Year, National Account Manager of the Year, six-time Presidents Club winner, and became the only sales and marketing executive to win the coveted President's Award in his division's history.

As a business leader Jeb has extensive experience building and developing sales organizations. He has a passion for growing people and the unique ability to see potential in everyone. Over the span of his career he has coached, trained, and developed thousands of salespeople and their leaders. Known for his ability to inspire others to action, he seeks to remove complexity from business situations, and instead focuses individuals and organizations on key actions that deliver quick and sustainable results.

As a keynote speaker, Jeb leaves audiences on the edge of their seats, wanting more. To have Jeb speak at your meeting or conference, please call 706-664-0810, email pby@salesgravy.com, or visit www.PeopleBuyYou.com.

1 | From Information to Empathy

What is most important to your success as a sales or business professional? Is it education, experience, product knowledge, job title, territory, or business dress? Is it your company's reputation, product, price, marketing collateral, delivery lead times, in stock ratios, service guarantees, management strength, or warehouse location? Is it testimonials, the latest *Forbes* write up, or brand awareness? Is it the investment in the latest CRM software, business 2.0 tools, or social media strategy? Is it your education, experience, work ethic, geography, business-card color, or connections?

You could hire a fancy consulting firm, make the list longer, add some bullet points, put it into a Power-Point presentation, and go through the whole dog and pony show. But at the end of the day there will be

only one conclusion... **None of the above**! You
see, the most important competitive edge for today's
business professionals cannot be found on this list,
your resume, or in any of your company's marketing
brochures.

If you want to know what your single most powerful competitive edge is, just look in the mirror. That's
right, it's you. Do these other things matter? Of course
they do, but these are just tickets that give you access
to the game. When all things are equal—and in the
competitive world we live in today they almost always
are—*people buy you*. Your ability to build lasting business relationships that allow you to close more deals,
retain clients, increase your income, and advance your
career to rise to the top of your company or industry,
depends on your skills for getting other people to like
you, trust you, and BUY YOU.

When you fully accept and adopt the *People Buy
You* philosophy, your confidence will go up and you
will perform at a higher level. You realize how very
powerful you can be as a business and sales professional
because, for the first time, you will understand just
how much you are in control of your destiny. You are
no longer tied to old paradigms. Things that you once
believed important are pushed to the wayside. Now
you know what really matters most in business is how
well you do in getting others to like you, trust you,
and believe in you. Once you wake up to the reality
that people buy *you,* real success and achievement are
within your grasp.

The Light Bulb Goes Off

I first sketched the outline for this book on a napkin while having lunch with a friend in San Francisco. We'd been discussing how utterly complicated most sales books and training had become over the past decade. As students of the sales profession, my friend and I had read hundreds of books on sales and business. As the publisher of the most visited sales web site on the planet, SalesGravy.com, I receive several new business books to review each week. It seems to me that each author tries to one-up the last with a new approach for sales and business success. I am continually amazed at the plethora of sales books, systems, and programs that claim to be the newest and greatest at helping sales professionals close more business, small business people reach nirvana by becoming big business people, leaders develop winning teams, and individuals build better careers. It is astonishing how confusing some of these books have made the process of doing business. The myriad new schemes more often than not ignore the basic principles of human interaction that drive everything in our lives.

My first sales manager taught me that selling is governed by basic rules and principles. While we worked together on complex, multi-million dollar deals, he coached me to focus intently on these basics at all times. Our closing percentage was among the highest in our industry, because we stuck to the basics. Over rarely strayed from these basics. Whenever I did, I was quickly reminded, by the gravitational force of failure, not to do it again. I know from experience as a sales professional, sales manager, and senior executive that it is enticing to think there is a magic pill solution to success. However, in business, it takes a keen and unwavering focus on the basics to sustain success year in and year out.

Twenty-First Century Trends

Some of the complexity and one-upmanship is being driven by three major trends: *technology, communication, and specialization.* Technology and communication have transformed and streamlined organizations, especially in larger companies. The art of business known to yesterday's generations is rapidly being replaced by a sleek process and system-driven science. Technology, communication, and specialization have forever altered the speed of business.

However, the major problem facing businesses today is that the pendulum of focus has swung too far toward technology, process, and systems, and too far away from the interpersonal skills. Many organizations have jettisoned the basics in favor of fads or focused so much on process and systems they have forgotten that, at the core, business is just one person helping to solve another person's problem. The irony is that huge

investments have been made in technology, communication, and systems for the express purpose of giving
their sales professionals and frontline employees more
time with customers, their support staff more time to
spend collaborating with each other, and their leaders
more time to spend with employees. It seems counterintuitive to me that companies would invest to give
their people more time to spend with other people
while turning their backs on teaching the basics of
interpersonal relationships.

The trend toward specialization also got my attention. Today more than ever, business professionals
have become specialists in their fields and industries.
Although there is still crossover, there is much less than
in the past. For example, it is very difficult for someone
in software sales to move into medical-device sales on
a whim. With the trend toward specialization, business professionals have to rely more on their personal
brands and relationships than at any other time in recent history. Their ability to rise, and stay at the top of
their industry and specialization will depend on their
flexibility to grow and adjust with industry changes,
to embrace technology and process, and, most importantly, to build lasting relationships. Building, foster-
ing, and tapping into your network, or *who*, to achieve
your career goal is one of the foundational themes
in Bob Beaudine's ground-breaking book, *The Power
of Who*. With training organizations focused so completely on systems and process, who will teach the next

generation of business people how to connect relationship skills to business process?

Meet Tim Sanders

Then I met Tim Sanders, the author of *The Likeability
Factor*. I had the unique opportunity to listen to his dy-
namic and engaging speech about likeability. It moved
me to action. Tim had it right! The more likable you
are, the greater the probability that you will be happier, healthier, and have more friends and success. As
a sales professional, I instantly began considering how
his *L-Factor* could be applied to the business of getting and keeping customers. What was the implication
to twenty-first century sales professionals? And, for
that matter, what was the implication for all business
professionals?

I believe at the granular day-to-day level, business
is just one person solving another person's problems.
Those one-on-one interactions repeated millions of
times, at all levels, each day are the gears that drive
business and the economy. Nowhere is this concept
more important than in sales. Sales is pretty simple:
solve your customer's problem and they will buy your
solution.

Thinking about business in this light was the tip-
ping point for the *People Buy You* project. I real-
ized that in the twenty-first century, interpersonal

relationships are more important than at any other time in our history. The paradox of technology is that it has removed barriers that for so long made communication slow, cumbersome, and expensive, while it has erected barriers that inhibit interpersonal interaction. In many ways we have moved into an era of instant communication and delayed response. Technology has removed the need to actually speak to other people or even meet with others face to face. These changes in the way we communicate have made it necessary for business professionals to learn and adopt new skills for building relationships, and they have placed more value on traditional relationship-building strategies.

A New Paradigm—from Information to Empathy

From the moment we entered the Information Age in the 1980s, process has been valued over people. The Internet and its accompanying technology wrung productivity out of every business process and system. As productivity per worker increased, so did our prosperity. As barriers to communication improved, we were then able to move the repetitive tasks that could be systematized overseas, where low wages helped boost profits even more. In less than two decades we removed human interaction from many of our day-to-day activities! Just consider how online banking and stock trading have changed the way we interact with our financial institutions. Along the way, customer service deteriorated at many companies as the service functions were moved online or overseas. You only need to reach a customer-service representative in another country who reads preapproved copy, like a robot, from her computer screen instead of actually helping you, to know how far the pendulum has swung.

Daniel Pink points out this phenomenon in his bestselling book, *A Brand New Mind*. He makes the case that workers who have the ability to be empathetic and interact with others will have the competitive and economic edge in the coming decades. Like Sanders and Beaudine, Pink makes us aware of the value of human interaction to our own success in both business and life.

We know intuitively that pendulums swing. Once the pendulum reaches its apex on one side, it stalls and rapidly gains momentum toward the other side. Now that the pendulum has reached its apex on the process side, human interaction, empathy, and interpersonal skills (previously devalued) are the new competitive edge for business and sales professionals. Jobs that can be boiled down to process have been shipped to other countries where cheap labor and technology do the work at a lower cost. The jobs that are left require human interaction and empathy. This is one of the reasons I continue to believe that sales is the most recession-proof and lucrative profession on earth.

What's the Point?

The objective of this book is simple. I want you to understand how important your ability to get others to like you, trust you, and buy you is to your future. Understand, though, that *People Buy You* is not about selling yourself. That is an old cliché, which, unless you are in the sex trade, is virtually meaningless. *People Buy You* is about interacting with others in a way that helps them get what they want so that you get what you want. It is about connecting with others for the express purpose of uncovering and solving their problems.

In this book you will not find long diatribes about human psychology and behavior. There won't be lessons on neuro-linguistic programming or understanding the intricacies of body language and facial expressions. I won't be quoting from textbooks about the studies of famous scientists. I will not provide tricks for manipulating others. This book is about action. It is about reality and the real world. *People Buy You* is a practical guide that will teach you easy, no nonsense steps that will instantly change how you are perceived by others, help you to develop lasting relationships, become more influential and persuasive, and ultimately allow you to gain the business success you deserve.

2

Friends Buy from Friends and Other Urban Myths

In sales and business there are a number of beliefs and clichés about relationships that are simply hyperbole. Trainers, sales managers, speakers, and authors love to use these sayings because they sound good and have been widely accepted as truth. As I explained in the first chapter, *People Buy You* is based on reality. The skills, concepts, and techniques taught in this book are actionable and can be employed immediately. No fluff. No feel good concepts that can't be executed in the real world. So before going further, I want to dispel three common relationship myths that are pervasive in sales and business and may be holding you back.

Myth #1: Friends Buy from Friends

In my early 20s I was hired by a company to be a sales representative. It was a commission only, business-to-consumer sales job that had very high turnover. But I was young, eager, and broke, so as I sat in the training room with the other new recruits, I couldn't wait to get started. Besides, because I was working my way through college, a sales job that allowed me to set my own hours and earn unlimited income seemed like a dream come true.

Our trainer was a guy named Jerry. He was fun and energetic. His job was to teach us the company's sales system, get us fired up, and send us out to sell. Within 30 days, the vast majority of our group would grow tired of the rejection, hit the wall, and quit. Jerry didn't tell us this fact. He told us that if we followed the system he taught us, we would soon be printing money.

Toward the end of our training, Jerry announced that we would have a special guest. The number one sales guy of all time was making a special trip to our class to share his secrets. All the young faces around me lit up. We all sat up in our seats and grabbed pen and paper. We were ready for the secrets to success.

Herb was a short, pudgy man who wore a cheap gray suit with brown scuffed-up shoes. To a 20-year-old, he looked ancient. He stood before our class and looked us over for a few minutes and said nothing.

We were in awe. There before us was the man who, according to Jerry, had broken every company record for sales. Herb delivered pleasantries: the best looking class of new salespeople he had seen in a long time, good to have us in the company, we would all do well. Then a serious look crossed his face and with a deep southern drawl he said, "Boys (there were no women dumb enough to sign up for this job), people often ask me why I'm so successful. I always tell them two things and you can take this to the bank. First, you've got to work hard. If you don't work hard you ain't gonna make any money. Second, and this is important (he paused for effect), friends buy from friends." And that was it. Herb's secret to success for selling replacement windows and siding was to work hard and sell to your friends.

The next day Jerry officially graduated us from sales training class. We all hit the streets looking for prospects. I remembered what Herb said so I called my friends and my parents' friends. A week later I was out of friends. It turned out none of them needed replacement windows or siding. I learned the lesson that countless real-estate agents, insurance agents, stock brokers, and network marketers have learned: only sometimes do friends buy from friends. Most times they do not, and it sure is easy to run out of friends or, more likely, watch them run from you.

Now some sales trainers say, "You just have to go out and make more friends." Well, I've got news for you, making new friends is not easy. It is inefficient and, frankly, you can only manage a finite number of friends in your life. Though it is true that your friends can and will help you get what you want, the vast majority of people you deal with in business will not, and never will be, your friends. If you want to succeed in business, you have to get the people who are not your friends to buy from you, too.

Myth #2: People Buy from People They Like

Several years later I attended a sales training class with a new company. I had just been hired as a sales representative selling business-to-business services. Our trainer stood before the class and exclaimed, "Just remember, people buy from people they like!" I wrote that down on an index card and taped it over my desk in the sales bullpen. Several weeks later a large prospect with whom I had developed a good relationship informed me that I was not getting his business. He said, "Jeb, we really like you and you did a great job with your presentation, but we've decided to go with your competitor."

I was devastated. All the signs I had gotten from the buyer indicated that I was going to get the deal. I had even told my sales manager that he could write it in stone—the deal was mine. I stammered back, "I don't understand, I thought I covered all the bases and gave you what you were looking for."

He responded, "Well, you missed a few things, and your competitor has a product that we think is better for our application. Like I said, we really like you and your presentation was excellent. It wasn't anything you did wrong. They just had a better solution for what we needed. If anything changes, I promise you'll be the first person we call."

Ouch! We had the exact same product but it turned out that the competitor had uncovered a problem I had failed to find. I lost several more accounts just like this before it started to get through my thick head that people don't necessarily buy from people they like. They buy from people who solve their problems. The issue was that I had substituted charm for substance. Don't get me wrong, it worked sometimes, which is why I continued to do it. The problem was, it did not work most times, and to be successful, I needed a better batting average.

Unfortunately, many people count on charm, charisma, and the gift of gab to pull them through. You certainly know these people. Some customers fall for the act, but most do not buy it. Eventually, these salespeople get the reputation for "All talk and no action." In Texas they say, "Big hat, no cows." My good friend and business partner calls these people "flippers and flappers," meaning they flip the pages of their presentations and flap their lips.

Being likable is critical if you want People to Buy You, but it is not enough. There is much more to the equation. This is what *People Buy You* is all about. *People Buy You* helps you get deeper than likability and opens up the door to connecting with and engaging others to uncover and solve problems, build trust, and anchor long-term relationships. It is not about selling or convincing, it is about connecting and solving.

A Truth: People Don't Buy from People They Don't Like

One truth you must be aware of is that people don't buy from people they do not like unless it is an absolute necessity (like buying ice in South Florida after a hurricane). One sales professional I interviewed, who is also one of the top sales professionals in her industry, has a rule of thumb. If she cannot connect with her buyer emotionally she will disengage from the sale and move on. She says that experience has taught her if the person she is dealing with does not like her for any reason, her chances of closing the sale are virtually zero no matter how well her package meets the buyer's needs.

Managers and business owners take note. Look around your business and think about it. Your customers buy your products and services and keep coming back to buy more because they like your employees. You must understand that when your customers begin to dislike your employees or you, they will quit coming back. Instead, they will find sales and service people who give them a feeling of emotional well-being about their purchase. Your salespeople, marketing, and advertising may get prospects emotional enough to buy once; but if they don't like the support team, customer-service reps, or others they deal with, you will lose them as customers in the long term.

Myth #3: You Have to Sell Yourself

Most of us, at one time or another in our careers, have heard some wise trainer or manager exclaim, *"You have to sell yourself."*

"If you want to get that job, son, you have to sell yourself."

"The real key to sales is your ability to sell yourself."

"If you want others to like you, you'll have to sell yourself."

This philosophy is prevalent in our business culture. Recently I was at an Ivy League University for a speech by a successful businessman to a group of MBA students from the top business schools in the world. The speaker was so well respected that when he walked into the room there was a hush. The audience members were on the edge of their seats in anticipation. And what was the message? What was the secret of success that this revered businessman offered? "Never forget how important it is in business to first sell yourself." The entire audience nodded in unison.

For this wise man and many others, the phrase *sell yourself* has become an easy-to-use cliché. It just rolls off the tongue. Like the audience at the speech I attended, most people will nod their heads in agreement to the statement as if some prophet on a hill had just read it from stone tablets.

Sales expert and bestselling author Jeffrey Gitomer teaches a simple philosophy, "People love to buy but they hate to be sold." In other words, most people prefer to buy on their terms. They do not want or appreciate a hard pitch or a features dump. Yet daily salespeople across the globe, either on the phone or in person, sell to their customers by dumping data, pushing their position, or simply trying to talk their way into a sale. Then, they go forth into the world and start selling at networking events, to clients, prospects, hiring managers, and anyone else they can get to stand still for more than five minutes.

But it does not work, because people like to buy, they don't like to be sold. The harder you try to sell yourself to others, the more you push them away. A conversation where the other person tells you all about themselves, their accomplishments, and how great they are is a turnoff. It is a features dump. You don't walk away from that conversation thinking how much you would like to spend more time with them. Instead you think, "What a jerk," or "How boring," or "Wow, that guy is full of himself."

Of course, we do love the opportunity to sell ourselves. Most of us, if given the opportunity, will talk for hours about our favorite person, oblivious to the negative impact it has on how we are viewed by others. When pressed, experts who are quick to tell you to sell yourself, are unable to explain exactly how to do it. Sure, they will offer tips, but they are mostly hyperbole. You cannot sell *yourself* to others; you have to get others to buy *you* on their terms. Even if you are preceded by a great reputation and others are anticipating meeting you, your attempts to sell yourself can backfire. I learned this lesson at a speech I gave to a large dinner group. One of the audience members was such a big fan of my book, *Power Principles,* that he lobbied the meeting organizer to be seated right next to me. During dinner he asked me questions, and I talked and talked and talked—about me. A few days after the speech, I called the meeting organizer to follow up and offer my thanks. I thanked him for seating Daniel next to me and asked him if Daniel had had a good time. He hesitated for a moment and finally said, "I'm telling you this because I like you; but Daniel did not come away with a very good opinion of you." It was like being punched in the gut! I responded that I thought that we had a great conversation and asked what went wrong. The meeting planner explained that Daniel felt that all I did was talk about myself. The truth hurts. I sold, but Daniel did not buy. People buy you for their reasons, not for your reasons. So when we sell people on why they should like us, it backfires. However, when they choose to buy you for their reasons, it creates a powerful connection and a relationship that makes almost anything possible.

People Buy You

This book teaches specific, actionable tactics you will be able to employ immediately to get people to buy you. *People Buy You* goes beyond myth and hyperbole and provides a framework for getting others to help you get what you want (i.e., purchase your product or service, give you a referral, hire you, promote you, etc.) by taking advantage of how people actually buy and make decisions.

One of the core principles at the foundation of the *People Buy You* philosophy is a universal law of human behavior: *People act first (or buy) on emotion and then justify those actions with logic.*

Every day as we go through life, we make hundreds of decisions. Some are big and some are small; some are made based on pure intuition; and others are considered until we feel good about our choices. Some people make decisions fast, and some people are slow to decide. Some weigh all of their choices, whereas others jump right in. Regardless, emotions guide them in advance of logic. No matter what empirical evidence they have before them, action is driven first by emotion. It does not mean that facts, numbers, observations, and statistics are not important. Evidence and supporting data are critical in decision making, but it is the emotion we feel that causes us to act.

Now, there are folks who will argue this point to the death. Unwilling to admit just how emotional we are as humans, they point to themselves as examples. They offer eloquent examples of how their decisions were made on facts and logic. In reality though, after a little questioning, I am always able to point to the fact that they have simply gone back and justified their initial emotional decision with logic. Hindsight is 20/20. We all do it. Business organizations realize that even the best purchasing managers, who are trained to buy based on facts and figures, are still swayed by emotion. In recent years a few purchasing departments have even begun holding online, reverse auctions. The aim? To take the human element—the emotions—out of the purchasing process.

At the core, sales and business is simply one person solving another person's problem. To solve someone's problem you must first get them to tell you what their problems are. You start by being **likable**. Being likable opens the door to an emotional **connection**. The more connected people feel to you, the more comfortable they feel sharing information that reveals their problems. With that information in hand you can focus on and **solve** their real **problems**. People are extremely loyal to people who solve their problems. However, even though your buyer might feel good emotionally about doing business, they are still looking for a foundation of logic with which to back up these feelings. Because of this, you must take careful steps to **build trust** through your actions and reinforce their emotional connection and trust in you with **positive emotional experiences**.

The Five Levers of *People Buy You*

I use the term *lever* because a lever is a simple tool that has the potential to produce tremendous force and move large objects. Archimedes said, "Give me a lever long enough and a fulcrum on which to place it, and I shall move the world." Likewise, the five levers of *People Buy You* work together to help you move others to action by tapping into motivations that are driven by human emotion.

Be Likable

Likability is the gateway to connections and ultimately to relationships. If others don't find you likable, then it is virtually impossible to form profitable business relationships. If you are not likable, people will not buy you or from you. Likability is responsible for first impressions because it happens in an instant, and it is responsible for ongoing impressions because it can be lost in an instant. When people find you likable, the door opens to emotional connections, to trust, and ultimately to business relationships that help you build a successful career and income.

Connect

Likability leads to connecting. Most sales texts and training programs describe this process as building rapport. Unfortunately, rapport as an action has become a box most salespeople simply check off as a step in the sales process. Unlike "Building Rapport" which can be manipulative and uncomfortable, connecting tears down walls that tend to get in the way of real communication and understanding. When people feel connected with you they feel more comfortable telling you their real problems. With this information in hand, you have the opportunity to solve problems that really matter. This provides real value and engenders true loyalty. Strong connections are hard to break and are the foundation of truly prosperous, long-term business relationships.

Solve Problems

One of the immutable laws of the universe is that when you give to others, you are rewarded tenfold. Problem solvers are the champions of the business world. However, it is impossible to solve problems you do not know about, which is why connecting is so critical. The essence of business is one person solving another person's problem. A solved problem is the value that buyers pay for. It is the most important lever in the *People Buy You* philosophy. The most successful business people take problem solving to the next level. These individuals are constantly on the lookout for problems they can solve—even if it has no direct impact on their business. They live by the motto, "By helping others get what they want, I will get what I want."

Build Trust

Trust is the glue that holds relationships together and the foundation on which all long-term relationships rest. Trust is developed with tangible evidence that you do what you say you will do, that you keep promises, and that you maintain a consistent commitment to excellence. It means going the extra mile in everything you do. In a world in which most people are doing just enough to get by, those business professionals who consistently do more than they have to will stand out. Buyers appreciate and reward this commitment to excellence with repeat business, referrals, and ultimately with trust.

Create Positive Emotional Experiences

Just as an anchor is used to hold a ship in place against currents, wind, tide, and storm, positive emotional experiences do the same for relationships. Positive emotional experiences anchor your relationships. They leave people wanting more of you. When you create positive emotional experiences for others, you take advantage of the law of reciprocity that opens the door for others to create positive emotional experiences for you, further anchoring and building relationships that will reward you for years to come.

Sales Tip

People Buy You is designed to teach you interpersonal skills that allow you to uncover and solve real problems. But there is one caveat. If you are building relationships

(continued)

(Continued)

with prospects that are not qualified (customers who for any reason don't have the ability to buy) or returning to the same prospects over and over again without adding new business, *People Buy You* will not benefit you. If your sales pipeline is empty or you are spending time with customers and prospects who are not qualified to buy, then you will not eat. I don't care how gifted you are at building relationships; in sales, activity drives everything—that's the law. Activity is the hard work of sales and it is the price you pay for your commission checks. Activities include: Cold calling, first-time visits, follow-up calls, product demonstrations, walk-throughs, test drives, site visits, open houses, tours, presentations, proposals, referrals, direct mail, and so forth. The fact is, if you have enough activity, you will at least sell something, even if you do everything else wrong. If you have no activity, but do everything else right, you will sell nothing. Of course, if your sales activity is consistent and you use the *People Buy You* levers, you will be a super star and your income will flourish.

3 | Be Likable

Brad stared out of the plate glass windows at the newly manicured landscaping around his new rental-equipment store. After 10 years of renting, he was finally in a building he owned. He was so proud of his accomplishment that he had invested in landscaping; the front of the store looked great. He relished the compliments from his regular customers. After years of hard work, he felt like he had finally made it.

Out in the parking lot, a late-model sedan pulled into one of the front parking spaces. A well-dressed woman, carrying a leather portfolio, climbed out of the driver's side. Brad surmised that this was his 10 A.M. appointment with the insurance agent he had called. Now that he owned his building, he needed to increase his liability coverage. As Brad was about to turn away to get the file with his current policy, which the agent had requested that he have ready for their meeting, he saw her drop her cigarette onto the pavement, stamp it out with her high-heel shoe, and kick it into the pine straw of his new landscaping. When Brad told me this story he said, "I felt an instant flash of anger. I couldn't believe what she had just done! I knew right then and there that I would never buy anything from her no matter what she presented."

In the meeting with the agent, Brad was cordial and never mentioned how he felt about the cigarette butt she had kicked into his landscaping. He thanked her for her presentation and proposal. Afterward, when she called the store to follow up, Brad was always unavailable or had no time to talk. Eventually she gave up calling, but she had no understanding of why she lost the sale.

Likability Is the Gateway to Connections

The word *likable* is defined by the Merriam-Webster Dictionary Online as, "having qualities that bring about a favorable regard." Being likable is not a guarantee that you will get the sale, promotion, or business deal. As we've already learned, it takes more than likability and charisma to win in business. Likability is, however, the first and most important step to get People to Buy You.

Of course, if you are unlikable people will not buy from you. In our People Buy You™ seminars, I always ask to see a show of hands from those who like spending time with unlikable people. I've never had a hand go up. The fact is, we do not enjoy being around people who are unlikable, and we avoid these people whenever possible. If you are not likable, others won't give you the opportunity to connect. In other words, if you are not likable you have virtually no chance to build a relationship.

Likability is the gateway to connections and relationships. We tend to be attracted to likable people and when we are likable, others are attracted to us. When people find you likable, the wall comes down just enough to allow for a conversation, which may lead to a connection and on to a profitable business relationship. Likability is also an integral part of maintaining and building the relationships you already have. If, at some point, your customer finds you unlikable, no matter the situation, your business relationship will eventually disintegrate.

People Buy You begins and ends with likability because being likable and remaining likable is sort of like "relationship glue." Likability impacts how others perceive you, their willingness to engage in conversation, and their openness to answering your questions. In addition, it affects their desire to give you second chances when inevitable mistakes and service issues occur. Likability makes the difference in how you and your message are received by others. Without it, you simply cannot and will not connect with others.

How to Be Likable

The cliché, "You never get a second chance to make a first impression," is an obvious play on words designed to illustrate the importance of first impressions. Like Brad, we all make instant judgments when we first meet people. Those judgments, which are both imperfect and emotional, have a lasting impact on how we view and interact with others. These same judgments are being made about us.

How long does it take for others to judge you as either likable or unlikable? An instant! Unlike trust, which is earned over time through many interactions, being perceived as likable or unlikable occurs in mere moments. So, when first meeting new prospects, customers, bosses, employees, and co-workers, it is critical that you control the behaviors that impact likability.

Some people are naturally likable. When they show up, the room lights up. They have appeal to a wide range of people. Others naturally gravitate to them and they make friends easily. These rare and gifted people, more often than not, have no idea why they are so likable. They have God-given talent and operate from pure instinct. They are naturally pleasant, have friendly facial expressions, and are talkative but not arrogant. We all, to some extent, have characteristics that make us naturally likable to others. We find it easy to connect with and develop relationships with certain types of people and personalities.

The problem we face in business, though, is that we don't always get to choose the people we interact with. This means that many of the people we encounter will not naturally be attracted to us. Complicating things are the preconceived perceptions that all people bring into relationships. These perceptions may include cultural, racial, and socioeconomic biases that are beyond our control.

There are, however, behaviors that are in our control. Behaviors, that make us more likable. These behaviors help us neutralize the biases and they open the door to connections and relationships with a wide range of people who might otherwise not find us likable.

Unless you have a natural God-given talent for being likable, you will have to work at and consciously practice these behaviors. Prior to meetings and interactions with others, you will need to remind yourself to practice likable behaviors. For example: if you are naturally more of an introvert, then you may have the tendency to feel insecure around strangers. This insecurity translates into behaviors like avoiding eye contact or displaying body language that suggests you lack confidence. To be more likable, you will have to overcome your natural instincts and, instead, make eye contact, pick your shoulders up, and smile confidently. The same goes for our many natural behaviors that impede likability. You must develop the self-discipline to remain consciously aware of your behaviors and be prepared to adjust those behaviors to the people with whom, and environments in which, you find yourself.

Is this easy? Well no; if it were, we would all seem more likable to one another. Changing natural behaviors is never easy, no matter what the endeavor. The vast majority of people in the world walk through life allowing their natural behaviors to negatively impact their current and potential relationships. These individuals are unwilling to make changes. Unfortunately, they are naively unaware of the impact this has on their success in sales, business, and life.

Likable Behaviors

The good news is that the stage is set for you to stand out in the crowd. As author Leanne Hoagland-Smith says, "You can be the red jacket in a sea of gray suits." The next piece of good news is that making changes to your natural behaviors is not only possible but also not nearly as hard as you may think.

Clearly, there are many things that influence likability. However, as I said, there are fundamental behaviors that universally impact likability, and these attributes are completely within our control. Smiling, good manners, being there, enthusiasm, confidence, and authenticity are behaviors that make you seem more likable to others. In the remainder of this chapter we will discuss how to leverage each of these key behaviors.

Smile

There is a saying, "Frown and you frown alone, but
smile and the whole world smiles with you." From
the moment we are born we learn that smiling is the
fastest way to get others to pay attention to us. A
baby's smile lights up the room. Smiles attract. Frowns
repel. Even dogs understand this. A wagging tail, an
upturned mouth, and bright, wide eyes are the fastest
route to a pat or treat.

Numerous scientific and psychological studies have
shown that the smile is a universal language that is
recognized across cultures and ethnicities around the
globe. Studies have also shown that smiling is social—
we smile far more with other people than we do
when we are alone. Smiling is a primary communication tool used to connect and bind us to others. The
smile has the ability to convey meaning depending
on its intensity. Excitement, humor, pleasure, confidence, happiness, welcome, love, understanding, caring, kindness, and friendship are all communicated
through the smile.

Though there are volumes of research on the importance of the smile in human behavior and communication, we don't need a researcher to explain
the obvious. The smile is the most effective way to
be likable. Period. We are attracted to people who are
smiling. We yearn to join groups of smiling people
because their smiles tell us they are happy and we want
to be happy. Smiles also set people at ease and create a

relaxed environment. Your sincere smile says, "I mean no harm. I'm open." In this more relaxed environment, you will find that people are more likely to talk to you, more willing to answer your questions, and more open to connecting and developing a relationship.

When you are smiling, people are more willing to help you. Gatekeepers and receptionists are more likely to give you information or connect you to a decision maker. People will offer you a hand. When you are smiling, people are more forgiving of mistakes and more understanding of your faults. A sincere smile humanizes business relationships and conveys authenticity.

Victor Borge once said, "The shortest distance between two people is a smile." There is simply no substitute for the smile when it comes to likability.

The Value of a Smile

He was smiling when he walked into the room. I was not. I was nervous, scared, and looking for any reason to walk out the door. Dr. Hampton was the third dentist I'd been to. I desperately needed some extensive dental work, except I have a phobia of dentists that defies logic. Unfortunately, I had avoided dentists for so long it was beginning to put my health in jeopardy. But, even in the face of this fact, after appointments with two other dentists, I never went back to them because I did not feel comfortable in their care.

I'd spent the morning working my way through the phone book calling dentists. On each call I tried to explain my irrational fear of dentists. In almost all cases this explanation was met with indifference. Then, I reached the receptionist at Dr. Hampton's office. I told her about my fear of dentists and asked a truly illogical question: "Is he painless?" She laughed out loud, and I could hear the smile in her voice when she gently told me that they had a lot of patients who were scared and that everyone loved Dr. Hampton. Her kind demeanor unwound my stress and I laughed with her. The morning before my appointment I began making excuses to cancel it, although I kept hearing the receptionist's kind voice saying "everyone loves Dr. Hampton," and I was able to will myself to his office.

When I walked in the office door, I was met with a smiling face that matched the smiling voice perfectly. Ann greeted me like an old friend. She even apologized to me for the stack of forms she handed me to fill out. To my amazement, she added that it shouldn't take long because she had already filled in my name, address, and insurance information. I couldn't remember the last time a business had taken the liberty to fill in their forms with the information they already had about me. I smiled back at Ann and thanked her for taking such good care of me.

As I filled out the forms I had a flashback to the last dentist I'd been to. The receptionist had barely looked up when I went to the small window that separated her from the patients stacked up in the waiting room. Once she had my name, she had handed me a stack of forms, and without another word closed the window behind her, leaving me to my own devices and ratcheting up my stress. At least at Dr. Hampton's office I felt welcomed.

A few minutes later, a dental technician walked into the waiting room and greeted me with a smile. She walked me back to the examination room. Then she said, "Ann said you are nervous. Don't worry, we'll take care of you, and everyone loves Dr. Hampton." Her smile was genuine. I was beginning to feel better, though still fighting the instinct to run. That's when I met Dr. Hampton. The minute he walked into the room, my heart started beating faster. Pain time! But Dr. Hampton had a disarming smile on his face. It was sincere and caring. I said, "I know it is irrational and I am a grown man; but I'm deathly afraid of dentists."

He dead-panned, "That's not irrational. If I were you I'd be afraid of me, too." Then he started laughing. I laughed and began to relax. His smile and the smiles of his staff disarmed my fear and made me feel that I was in good hands.

Was Dr. Hampton painless? Hell, no. He hurt me. The repairs to my teeth were expensive and time-consuming. But he and his staff acknowledged my feelings and treated me with kindness and respect. I kept all my subsequent appointments, though, and I was always greeted with a smile. To this day, Dr. Hampton is the only dentist I trust to work on my teeth. He gained a good customer in me (I'm sure I've paid for one of his kids' college tuition) all because of a good sense of humor and a genuine smile.

People Respond in Kind

Take a look around you. Notice how few people are smiling? Now try this experiment. When they look up at you, smile at them. I've found that nine out of ten times they will smile right back. When that happens—you smile at them and they smile at you—for just a moment you have an instant connection.

When it comes to likable behaviors such as smiling, politeness, respect, and kindness, people tend to respond in kind. Savvy customer service and account management professionals use this to their advantage with angry and upset customers. No matter how rude or angry the customer is, they remain calm, respectful, and pleasant. In almost all cases the customer calms down, and in many cases will apologize for their behavior.

People respond in kind. When you are polite, they tend to be polite. When you are respectful, it is likely you will receive respect in return. And when you smile, most people will smile back at you.

Because people respond in kind, you have the opportunity to control the tone of most of your interactions with others. Instead of being at the mercy of circumstances, you can influence the emotions prospects and customers feel when meeting with you by simply managing your own behaviors. How simple is it? Well, we know that smiling makes us feel good. That is why we like to smile. When you smile, others will smile with you. Once they begin smiling they feel good. When your actions make your prospects and customers feel good, they will naturally find you more likable.

Why Don't People Smile?

Take a walk through your company's offices, the mall, down the street, in public places, and look around. You will notice many dour, serious faces. Call businesses and ask for customer service, and you'll hear few smiling voices. Why then, if smiling is such an important part of human communication and it feels good to smile, are so few people smiling?

The simple answer is they are thinking about something else—usually themselves.

In social situations smiling comes naturally in response to others. It is innate, instinctual, and automatic. When someone says something funny or greets us with a smile, we smile back. But when we are not prompted to smile by the people around us, it is natural for our attention to revert back to our own problems and ourselves.

The fact is, you are thinking about yourself as much as 95 percent of the time. When you are not thinking about yourself you are usually thinking about a problem or obstacle that is in the way of you thinking about yourself. In other words, when people are not smiling, it is, most often, not because they are unhappy, but rather because they are lost in thought. Unfortunately, when you are lost in your own thoughts you are not that likable. This is not such a problem for a mailroom clerk or a bookkeeper, but it is a big deal for salespeople, account managers, customer-facing employees, managers, and executives who depend on relationships with others.

Put a Smile on Your Face

It is natural to be lost in thought and focused on your own wants and needs. As you walk into appointments with a client, you may be thinking about what you are going to say, your last call, the boss, the deal you just lost, a customer service issue, the strange noise your car just made, or your kid's next little league game. But as you walk into your client's business, all eyes are on you. What will they see? How will people perceive you? Will they see a smiling, upbeat, and likable business professional or a serious, self-absorbed, unapproachable person? You control these perceptions, and perceptions have a tremendous impact on your likability.

Because smiling is not a natural state outside of social situations, you must consciously make the effort to put a smile on your face when meeting others or when picking up the phone. The key words here are *conscious* and *effort*. Making a conscious effort means:

- Being aware of where you are and those around you.
- Pushing your own thoughts aside.
- Putting a smile on your face even if initially you have to fake it.

Smiling in social situations is easy; doing it in the real world so that it appears spontaneous and sincere takes practice. A technique some people use to smile naturally and sincerely is to just think of something pleasant. This has the added benefit of lifting your mood. It is easier to smile when you feel good and are thinking about happy things. Thinking about something pleasant also helps you relax and improves your confidence—two keys to smiling naturally. I like to look in the mirror before I walk in to see a prospect or customer (or get on the phone) and practice smiling. If I'm in the parking lot of my next appointment I'll look in the rearview mirror and smile—big and wide. It looks ridiculous. But by the time I walk into the building, I'm greeting everyone from the security guard, to the receptionist, to my client, with a pleasant, friendly smile. And because people respond in kind, it doesn't take long for the people I meet to smile back at me.

Take a moment and consider the last time someone greeted you with a big smile. Chances are, it made you feel great. You knew they were glad to see you and it made you happy to see them. That is one of the best things about a smile. Dale Carnegie put it best, "When you greet people with a smile you'll have a good time meeting them and they'll have a good time meeting you."

Be Polite, Nice, Respectful, and Mind Your Manners

When I was a kid and we would go places, my mother would sit us all down and sternly remind us to *mind our manners*. My brothers and sisters and I were not perfect, but eventually with the firm guidance of our mother we learned etiquette and how to behave properly around others. Most people, at some point in their lives, have been taught the same basic manners and etiquette. Almost everyone knows right from wrong, the difference between being rude and polite, and how to be respectful of others. Yet, as illustrated in the opening story of this chapter; many people *choose* to be self-centered and focused only on themselves and their own needs.

Have you noticed how many mean, nasty, ill man-
nered, rude, and disrespectful people there are in the
world today? It seems like rude people are everywhere.
Rudeness and impolite behavior have become so
prevalent that often it is just accepted as normal. I once
saw a bumper sticker that read, "Mean People Suck."
How true! No one really wants to be around people
who are rude and lack manners. No one says, "Did you
see how rude John was? What a jerk! I hope he comes
by again soon so we can spend more time with him."
Rude, impolite people are not likable. In sales and
business, failure to adhere to basic manners and rules
of etiquette will damage your career and your income.

With so many impolite people walking around,
there is a real opportunity for polite, nice business
people to make a great impression. These days, good
manners seem so rare that when you are consistently
kind and polite to those around you, people notice and
remember you. Good manners are appreciated, make
you likable, and in today's world give you a definitive competitive edge. Fortunately, being polite and
demonstrating good manners and etiquette is completely within your control. All you need is a little
self-discipline to focus on those around you rather than
on yourself. Use the Golden Rule as your guide. Just
treat others the way you would like to be treated. This
means everyone from the janitor to the CEO. Being
polite only to people that matter demonstrates lack

of character and is disingenuous. Besides, you never know who is watching.

Be Nice

At my company, SalesGravy.com our values statement says, *"We will be kind to everyone, no matter what."* Salespeople in particular have the reputation for being pushy, and especially so with gatekeepers and support staff. Many customer-service people and account managers have gained the reputation of being short and rude to customers. Being nice does not mean that you can't be assertive. You do not need to roll over in order to be kind. It does mean that talking down to other people, being overly demanding, demonstrating impatience, and generally showing a lack of kindness all conspire to damage your likability and credibility. You should never forget that someone you have been less than kind to may be just the person you will need help from in the future. When dealing with others, practice being cheerful, polite, calm, respectful, and appreciative, no matter how they treat you. Treat others the way you want to be treated. More often than not, people will respond in kind. Take our motto as your own. Be kind to everyone, not matter what. I guarantee that your reputation as a professional will grow in the wake of your kindness.

Compliment Others

Abraham Lincoln said, "Everyone likes a compliment." I once worked for a man who had a habit of complimenting everyone he met. He was an executive running a two-billion-dollar-a-year business—the big boss. He traveled the country visiting his company's offices and production facilities. Wherever he went, the people at his plants looked forward to his visits. Everyone from the part-time worker picking up trash in the parking lot to the top managers received a sincere compliment whenever he was around. They would kill for this man. Anything he asked for would be done. Not because they had to do it, but because they wanted to do it.

One of the easiest ways to be likable and win others over is to offer a sincere compliment. Developing awareness of others will help you notice things about them to compliment. The key is to put your own self-centered thoughts aside and become genuinely interested in other people. When you give people a genuine, sincere compliment about a trait, possession, or accomplishment, you've given them a valuable gift. You make them feel valued, acknowledged, and important. Most important, when people feel this way, their self-esteem goes up, they like themselves more, and because of this, they find you likable.

When I smile and others respond in kind, I like to compliment them with, "You have a great smile." Each time I do this their grin gets even bigger. Compliment, clothes, handsome kids, awards, children's artwork, or personal traits. If you know the person well or have done research in advance of meeting them, compliment an achievement. The key is training yourself to be interested and observant of others. When you do, you will be amazed at how far a sincere compliment takes you.

Be Respectful

According to Wikipedia,

> **Respect** *denotes both a positive feeling of esteem for a person or other entity (such as a nation or a religion), and also specific actions and conduct representative of that esteem. Respect can be a specific feeling of regard for the actual qualities of the one respected (e.g., "I have great respect for her judgment"). It can also be conduct in accord with a specific ethic of respect. Rude conduct is usually considered to indicate a lack of respect, whereas actions that honor somebody or something indicate respect.*

Respect and manners go hand in hand. I grew up in the South where we were taught that it is proper to address those older than you or in a position of authority with "Yes, sir" and "No, sir" and "Yes, ma'am" and No, ma'am." Although I realize that this is a regional and cultural practice isolated to the American South, because this practice so clearly demonstrates respect, it has served me well all over the world because it is a tangible demonstration of my respect. The same goes for "please" and "thank you." Show your gratitude and it will not go unnoticed.

You can show respect in many ways. Standing up when someone walks into a room is a sign of respect. Shaking hands and making eye contact demonstrates respect. Walking on the sidewalk rather than through your client's landscaping is a sign of respect. Asking permission to sit down, to set something on your prospect's desk, or walk around to the other side of their desk are all signs of respect. Respect is waiting your turn to speak, being appreciative for help that is given, and waiting for others to be served before eating at business meals.

Respectful people are very likable and usually receive respect in return. The key to consistently showing respect is turning off your self-centered thoughts and instead focusing on others. It is awareness of those around you and how your actions impact them. It is also a product of your character, integrity, and belief that showing and demonstrating respect is the right thing to do. Consistently showing respect for others is one of the fastest tracks to promotions, pay raises, customer retentions, increased sales, and likability.

Sales Tip: The Secret Lives of Gatekeepers

Earlier this year while I was training my new assistant and reviewing her responsibilities, she asked me how she should handle calls from salespeople. By the look on her face I could tell that dealing with salespeople wasn't a task she liked. It made me think about the ongoing tug-of-war between sales professionals, who are trying to get in the door, and the legions of gatekeepers assigned the duty of keeping them at bay.

I also considered that with so many people vying for my time, both inside and outside of my organization, if I met with every salesperson who called, I would never get my job done, which is exactly why I have a gate-keeper. My assistant's most important job is to protect my time so that I remain focused on the most critical tasks of my business. Unfortunately, that puts her in the unenviable position of saying no to salespeople, which, ironically, keeps a large cadre of authors, consultants, and speakers in business, creating libraries of books, audio programs, and DVDs designed to teach you the secrets to getting around gatekeepers.

A universal truth in sales is that salespeople hate gatekeepers. These blockers stymie their sales efforts and keep them from getting to decision makers who can say yes to deals. The difficulty in getting past gatekeep-ers is so frustrating that many times good salespeople

(*continued*)

(*Continued*)

just give up. Because they don't know how to deal with gatekeepers, many sales professionals become so frustrated that they begin to experiment with tricks that, too often, make them look foolish. These schemes are why so many gatekeepers, like my assistant, would rather have their teeth pulled out than deal with a salesperson.

So, is there a secret? I know you are hoping I'll say yes, but the answer is no. There are no secrets or magic pills that will get you past gatekeepers. The brutal reality is that in sales, only a select few will ever get through the gates. But it is critical to understand that gatekeepers are people just like you. They have emotions, worries, motivations, and, like you, a boss and a job to do. Because of this, your success in getting through the gate depends on a combination of good manners, likability, and savvy business acumen.

Project a positive, cheerful, outgoing personality. Be polite and respectful. You are guaranteed to fail with gatekeepers if you are rude, pushy, or ill-mannered. Always leave them with a positive impression of you and your company.

Use *please,* please. In the book, *The Real Secrets of the Top 20 Percent,* the author, Mike Brooks, advises that the single most powerful technique to get past gatekeepers is to use *please* twice. For example, when a gatekeeper answers the phone you might say, "Hi, this is Jeb Blount from SalesGravy.com. Could you please connect me to Bill Jenkins, please?" Using *please* twice is powerful, and it works because it shows respect and good manners.

Always provide full information about yourself. Tell the gatekeeper who you are, your full name, and the name of your company. To do otherwise creates a big neon sign with an arrow pointing to you that says, "pushy salesperson." Full disclosure makes you sound professional and like someone worthy enough to pass through to the boss.

Gatekeepers are people just like you. And like you, they like people who are interested in them. If you speak to a particular gatekeeper often, be sure to ask about how they are doing. Learn to listen to their tone of voice and respond when you hear something amiss. Ask questions about their family and their interests. There are gatekeepers I deal with on a regular basis whom I know better than the boss. When I call I will often spend more time talking to them than to my client. Because of these strong relationships, they take care to ensure that my call always takes priority, that I get on calendars, and they go out of their way to help me secure more business.

Never use cheesy schemes or tricks. Tricks don't work. They harm your credibility and you'll end up on the gatekeeper's do-not-talk-to list, which means it will

(continued)

(Continued)

have to snow at the equator before you get through. Be honest about who you are and why you are calling and ask for what you want. You may not get through the first time, but your honesty will be appreciated and remembered, which will play a huge role in opening the gate in the future.

Be There

In today's demanding work environment, it is easy to become distracted. BlackBerries, iPhones, and mobile computing leave us constantly looking at our devices. Cell phone calls interrupt conversations. E-mail and the Internet distract us while we are on the phone. The late Jim Rohn said, "Wherever you are, be there." This is essential advice when it comes to interpersonal relationships and likability. You must develop the self-discipline to shut everything else out and remain completely focused on the person in front of you.

Failing to focus on the person you are interacting with is a fast track to becoming unlikable. If you've ever been in a conversation with another person and they look away, get distracted by something or someone else, or interrupt your conversation with them to return a text message or e-mail, you know how disrespected this makes you feel. When you don't feel like the other person is listening to you, it hurts your feelings, makes you feel unimportant, and in some cases it makes you mad. When you are interacting with a prospect, customer, employee, staff member, or any other person, be there. Turn everything else off, remain completely focused, and do not let anything distract you.

Be Enthusiastic and Confident

Enthusiasm and confidence go hand in hand because both are external manifestations of inward beliefs, feelings, and attitudes. Enthusiasm for your product, service, company, or industry, and confidence in yourself and ability to deliver on your promises are highly likable traits. Enthusiasm in the right measure is infectious. Confidence in the right measure provides others with a sense of security that you know how to solve their problems.

Be Enthusiastic

Enthusiasm is simply having excitement for or interest in what you are doing. What we have already learned about human nature is that people respond in kind. If you are enthusiastic about something, it is likely that those around you will become enthusiastic, too. The good news is we generally find enthusiastic people likable, and we are more likely to accept their point of view. This is why enthusiasm is such an important tool for salespeople. There is an old saying, "A salesperson without enthusiasm is just a clerk."

The question that always arises when discussing enthusiasm is, "How do I become enthusiastic about a product, service, idea, or company that does not excite me?" First, you have to realize that the vast majority of people in business do not work in glamorous industries or with glamorous products. Of course some people work for companies like Apple where it is easy to get enthusiastic about the cool products. But most of us work for companies in which the products and services are mundane. The key here is to find something to become enthusiastic about. I've got a good friend who sells conveyer belts. He makes well into the six figures—one of the top salespeople in his industry. He's been selling conveyer belts for almost 20 years. Knox loves what he does. His enthusiasm is effusive. It is not the conveyer belts that get him excited though. He loves working with his customer base. He is enthusiastic about finding solutions to his customers' diverse set of problems. One of the fastest ways to become enthusiastic is to learn to appreciate the things about your company, product, service, or career that excite you. Train yourself to look for and find the positives in every situation and focus on those things.

If there is absolutely nothing about your situation that you can be enthusiastic about, I suggest you find something else to do quickly. Prospects, customers, managers, and peers can tell when you lack enthusiasm. As Vince Lombardi famously said, "If you are not fired with enthusiasm, you will be fired with enthusiasm." It is likely, though, that things will not get that bad and all you need to do is prime the enthusiasm pump. That means you might have to fake it til' you make it by demonstrating the enthusiastic attitude that you would like to create. In other words, you might have to pretend for a while—play the part. Dale Carnegie said that when you act enthusiastic you become enthusiastic. It works this way because when you act in a certain way long enough, subconsciously those actions eventually define who and what you become.

Be Confident

One of the most important, and sometimes overlooked, keys to getting people to buy you is your confidence. Just think about it, do you enjoy being around people who lack confidence? Neither do your prospects and customers.

Self-confidence is a balance. On one end of the spectrum there are those who lack any confidence. These weak people are unlikable and ineffective in most endeavors. On the other end of the spectrum there is overconfidence. Arrogant people, though sometimes successful, are turn-offs and eventually crash and burn. Confident people are very likable. We like to be around and associated with confident people because confident people look successful. Confidence is driven by your self-image, product knowledge, attitude, the way you dress, your health, and even your spirituality. Your level of confidence naturally goes up or down depending on specific situations. However, confident people have an underlying belief in themselves that transcends situational issues. It is this self-confidence that empowers them to be adaptable to the unpredictable environment around them.

This core confidence is a belief that no matter what happens, they will find a way to succeed. Perhaps the best description of this underlying belief was Henry Ford's often quoted line, "Whether you think you can or you think you can't, you are right." Your aptitude for developing confidence plays a critical role in your sales career. Unfortunately, as you well know, confidence is a complicated emotion involving many internal and external influences. Regardless, you can learn to develop and maintain confidence. However, it will take time and persistence. There will be many ups and downs. In fact, at times you will feel like you are in a catch 22. For example, if you are in a slump, your confidence will naturally erode even though you will be required to regain your confidence to have any chance of emerging from your slump. Just ask any major league slugger or sales professional whose batting average has dipped and they will explain.

The good news is you have the power inside you right now to develop confidence, even if you don't feel particularly confident at this moment. The process of improving or building your confidence is as simple as your choices. You choose what to believe about yourself and your abilities. You choose how you will approach other people. You choose to improve your product and industry knowledge. You choose to invest in yourself—mind, body, and spirit.

What do you believe about yourself and your ability to succeed? What are you afraid of? It is easy to find out. Just listen to your self-talk. Above all things, your self-talk has more impact on your confidence than anything else. You talk to yourself constantly. This ongoing internal conversation will either lift you up, giving you courage and confidence, or pull you down. If you are saying negative things to yourself that are eroding your confidence, then you are just creating your own problems and you have got to stop.

Fear, uncertainty, and doubt are the reasons for most negative self-talk. World War I ace, Eddie Rickenbacker, was quoted as saying that "Courage is doing something you fear." He also said that courage cannot exist without fear. Rickenbacker believed that fear was natural and that it was overcoming fear that created courage. He believed that it was alright to feel afraid, but it was just not alright to allow fear to hold you back. The people who develop courage and learn to be courageous, over time, reap the most success and rewards.

Developing courage rather than running away from fear helps you improve your confidence. Rickenbacker had it right. Fear is a requirement for courage. When you learn to use fear to systematically practice and build a strong foundation of courage, over time your self-confidence becomes unwavering. The secret is using fear, like a body builder uses iron to create muscle mass, to exercise and build your confidence.

When a body builder first starts working out, he uses light weights. Slowly, day after day, repetition after repetition, he adds weights until soon he is lifting two, three, or four times as much as when he started. In this same way you can build a strong foundation of courage and confidence. Just take small steps. There is certainly no way to overcome all of your fears. However, when you make it your mission to overcome one or two things you fear each day, you'll make real progress. Keep track of your accomplishments to build your self-confidence. Soon, a little bit each day, your confidence will grow stronger.

Invest in Yourself

Maintaining a confident and enthusiastic demeanor is difficult in the brutal business environment of the twenty-first century. Technology and communication have increased the speed of business and leveled the playing field among competitors. The pace of business in today's environment is faster than at any time in the human experience. This is especially true for those working in the sales profession. The pressure to sell and the demand to perform is unrelenting. You must deliver results or be fired. Companies demand more productivity, shorter sales cycles, and higher margins. Miss your numbers and you are out. Exceed them and you are a hero. You are no longer judged by what you have done, but rather what you have done today. The mental and physical toll on hard-working sales and business professionals can be brutal.

On a typical day, most salespeople get started in the wee hours of the morning. Many have to get their families ready for the day before they can even start thinking about sales activity. You may even be a single parent juggling the responsibilities of parenthood and a full-time sales job.

Once you get to the office, you start your sales day by prospecting and following up on leads. Prospecting generates many no's, and each no, each rejection, saps your confidence.

Then you go to appointments, you make presentations, you tour facilities, you ask questions, you gather information, you give product demonstrations and showings, you endure conversations with your customers at lunches and dinners, you give proposals, and you close deals. Sometimes you hear, "Yes."

Many times you hear, "Maybe." But because you are in sales, more often than not, you hear, "No, no, no." Every no steals a little bit of your confidence and enthusiasm.

Finally, after a day of battle on the streets, you come back to the office and fight for your customers. You remove road blocks, deal with negative people, and fix problems. You deal with back orders. You answer to the boss. You fight the office. You fight for contract approvals, for credit approvals, and many times for commissions or bonuses. Every problem, every roadblock affects your attitude.

At the end of the day you go home. You deal with your spouse, your kids, your pets, your neighbors, the bills, and a million other things. Your energy is drained, your belief system deteriorates, and the stress takes a physical toll.

All of these things and more conspire to eat away at your confidence and enthusiasm. To combat this, you must take steps to invest in yourself: *mind, body, and spirit*. To remain confident and enthusiastic you must take time to reenergize and build your positive attitude.

Invest in Your Mind

Gandhi said, "We should live as if we will die tomorrow and learn as if we will live forever." I've observed that business professionals who continually exercise their intellect are happier, more motivated, more confident, and, invariably, more likable than their peers. They take advantage of every training program their company offers and are always the first people standing in line when there is an opportunity to learn something new. They invest their own money in seminars and workshops to keep their skills updated and sharp. They read constantly and are rarely caught without a book. They subscribe to weekly e-zines, trade magazines, and business publications to stay current on their industry. These professionals understand that by investing in the mind, they acquire the knowledge and skills that improve their confidence and problem solving skills.

Invest in Your Body

Sales and business is a mental game. Thinking requires a tremendous amount of energy. Your mental energy is limited by your physical energy, so becoming physically fit naturally boosts mental energy. Major studies have proven that regular exercise improves creative thinking, mental clarity, and the capacity to bounce back from inevitable rejection. Being physically fit also makes you look good. When you look good, you feel good. Prospects and customers judge you by your physical appearance. They want to do business with winners, and winners look and feel confident.

Invest in Your Spirit

I've interviewed hundreds of business executives on the subject of spirituality. At the core, these highly successful people, all from different backgrounds, believe that there is something or someone bigger than themselves working in their lives. They believe that everything in life is connected, and they have faith that everything happens for a reason. They believe that a higher good is looking out for them and wants abundance in their lives. They believe that the spirit requires nourishment, exercise, and constant attention.

Investing in your spirit is, in essence, an investment in a strong belief system. Your belief system determines your attitude, perspective, and confidence. For instance, if like the successful people mentioned in the preceding paragraph, you believe that everything happens for a reason, your perspective and attitude on potentially negative events will be optimistic. Instead of whining, "Why me?" you ask, "How can I learn from this?" Your beliefs have a direct impact on your confidence, enthusiasm, likability, and, ultimately, on the quality of your relationships.

Authenticity

In business situations it is often tempting to pretend to be someone or something you are not. When you feel this temptation, it is your ego speaking. It is a desire to rise above your lack of self-confidence by being misleading or phony. Insecurity is at the heart of a lack of authenticity. Negative self-talk and the subconscious belief that you are not good enough tempt you to say or do things to compensate for these feelings. Most people are gifted with the intuition to see right through this. They know when things do not seem to add up or if you seem fake. Once they do, your trustworthiness and integrity are immediately in question, which diminishes your ability to connect. Think about it. When people are not authentic with you, how do you feel?

Authenticity is the child of confidence. When you develop and maintain self-confidence, you overcome the temptation to pretend to be something or someone you are not in order to stroke your own ego. You have enough trust in yourself to "keep it real" and be yourself. In terms of likability, being yourself equals being human, which is far more likable than many people suppose. It is also easier because it does not require effort to tell the truth.

Of course, business settings require a higher level of professionalism. In these situations, being yourself does not mean acting the way you would with a bunch of your college buddies. Manners, respect, and etiquette remain important. You will need to balance being a real human being with interpersonal skillfulness that allows you to be sensitive and diplomatic.

Turning First Impressions into Lasting Impressions

It is important to note that likability can be fleeting. In new relationships, first impressions are turned into lasting impressions when your behavior remains consistent. A rude remark, an inconsiderate act, a slip in your confidence, or losing your temper can quickly turn positive first impressions into lasting negative impressions. In business relationships, you must never forget that you are always on stage and being observed by others. In an imperfect world with imperfect personalities and unpredictable circumstances, you must employ self-discipline and vigilance to ensure that you consistently manage the elements of likability that remain in your control.

Of course, the longer and more connected your relationship becomes, the more forgiveness and leeway you will be given. This does not mean you can take these relationships for granted. In business, that is the fastest way to lose. The same actions that helped you make a good first impression, repeated again and again, keep these relationships anchored and profitable. We'll explore anchoring in greater detail in Chapter 7.

Summary

Likability is the gateway to connecting. Successful business professionals are likable. They are cheerful, polite, and demonstrate a positive, confident, attitude. They feel good about themselves and believe that they have the ability to solve their clients' problems. They know they are good at what they do, and their customers know it as well. Because of these likable qualities, their prospects and customers are open to connecting, and these connections lead to long-term profitable relationships.

4 | Connect

When Jennifer was in her sophomore year of college she decided to join her school's student-newspaper staff as an advertising salesperson. As a business major, she thought the experience would be a valuable addition to her budding resume. The paper paid a small commission for advertising sales that she hoped would provide some spending money.

On her first day, she met with the editor to discuss advertising accounts. During the meeting she asked about the Ford dealership that was near campus. The editor just shook his head and said, "Don't waste your time there. The owner of the dealership got mad at us a few years back and won't buy any more ads." After the meeting with her editor, Jennifer defiantly marched right over to the dealership and asked for the owner.

"I hate it when people tell me that something is impossible. All I could think was there had to be a way to get a big dealership that was so close to campus to buy an ad in our newspaper. The owner of the dealership was willing to see me, and an hour later I walked out with an ad order. It really was easy," she told me matter-of-factly.

I had met Jennifer at a cocktail party after a speech I gave to her company. Jennifer's manager introduced her to me as one of the best salespeople in the company. She had a cheerful personality and was instantly likable. She told me this story after I'd asked about how she had decided on a career in sales. Like most top sales professionals, she just ended her story by telling me how easy it was to do something others, like her editor at the newspaper, found impossible. I pressed her for the details.

"Wait a minute," I said. "You walked into a business that no one else on the newspaper staff could close, where the owner was reportedly mad, and you walked out with a deal—on your first day? That's unbelievable! There's got to be more to this story. What happened in that meeting exactly?"

She shrugged her shoulders. "I just let him talk."

"What specifically did you talk about?" I asked.

"We talked about him," she finally said. "For most of the meeting he told me why he had gotten so mad at the newspaper. He said that they weren't responsive and didn't show his dealership the respect he thought it deserved. He vented and I just listened to him. He was agitated at first but he calmed down. He told me that he really wanted to advertise with the paper because the students were good customers for used cars, but no one had ever come by to talk to him about it again, and he had been too mad to call.

"I responded, 'It isn't fair the way you've been treated by my newspaper. Your dealership was such an important account for the newspaper and you deserved more attention.' Then I asked, 'What if I was your main contact and if you needed anything you could just call me?'"

"He started grinning and said, 'I like you.'"

"He said he would buy more ads as long as he could just deal with me. Then, he gave me his order. When I got back to campus and showed the editor, his mouth dropped open."

As I considered her story I thought to myself, "That's *People Buy You*." The owner of the dealership didn't buy the paper, a sales pitch, or price. He bought Jennifer because she was likable, listened to him, made him feel important, and solved his problem.

Real Connections

Most everyone has at least one person in his or her life with whom there is a real lasting connection. These connected relationships are usually with spouses, best friends, or family. These connections are characterized by descriptions like, "She is someone I can talk to about anything." Or "He knows all about me—all my secrets." When you have problems in your life, these are the people you go to first for help because you know they will listen. Because they listen, you feel that you can reveal what is really happening—your real feelings and problems—instead of hiding them as you do with others.

Of course these types of connections are personal and different from business relationships. However, the principles are the same. In all relationships—business and personal—the more connected you feel to another person, the more you are willing to reveal your true feelings and problems. As I've said before, at the core, business is simply one person solving another person's problem. The challenge is uncovering problems to solve. Unless people feel some sort of connection with you, they will be reticent to tell you their real problems and to reveal their emotions relative to those problems. Just as likability is the gateway to connections (and for that matter all relationships), connecting opens the door to problem solving—and ultimately trust.

The Problem with Rapport

The Merriam-Webster dictionary online defines *rapport* as *relation marked by harmony, conformity, accord, or affinity.* According to Wikipedia,

Rapport is one of the most important features or character-istics of unconscious human interaction. It is commonality of perspective: being "in sync" with, or being "on the same wavelength" as the person with whom you are talking. There are a number of techniques that are supposed to be benefi-cial in building rapport such as: matching your body language (i.e., posture, gesture, and so forth); maintaining eye contact; and matching breathing rhythm. Some of these techniques are explored in neuro-linguistic programming.

Rapport is a popular and ubiquitous concept in sales. A module on rapport is included in virtually every sales and leadership training course. You'll find chapters on rapport in almost every sales book. Hundreds of books and seminars are dedicated exclusively to the concept of rapport. A search on Google for how to build rapport yields a million or so returns. Despite all of this, rapport is among the most misunderstood and misapplied concepts in business. Ask 10 salespeople to explain rapport and you'll get 10 different answers. Few people really understand the concept.

Rapport is essentially being in sync with another person to the extent that you are able to influence their behavior. The rapport building process is designed to develop common ground with another person through mirroring and matching body language, voice tone and speed, word patterns, eye movement, and even breathing. In time, according to the experts, when you truly have rapport with someone, you have the ability to lead them and change their behavior patterns. A process called neuro-linguistic programming (NLP), which embodies these techniques, including word-pattern matching, eye movement, facial expressions and more, is espoused by many rapport experts as the real key to relationships and influence.

The problem with rapport is that it is just too hard and complex to get into sync with someone enough to influence their behaviors. I'm not saying it is impossible for those willing to dedicate themselves to years of practice to become competent in NLP techniques. However, the reality is, despite promises from experts, these techniques are far too complicated for normal people. Few business professionals have the time or inclination to become experts in deciphering word patterns, eye movements, and facial expressions. Learning to effectively and discretely mirror and match people based on their communication style—audio, visual, or kinesthetic—sounds really cool in a seminar, but it rarely succeeds consistently in real world business situations with real people.

This doesn't mean that finding common ground is a bad thing. Far from it. The more we have in common with others, the easier it is for them to like us. If you find common ground, use it to your advantage to connect with the other person. The dilemma is that the quest for common ground in the guise of rapport building is often awkward, cheesy, and manipulative. Making matters worse are the legions of salespeople who mistake small talk at the beginning of a sales call as rapport building. Taking their cue from misinformed sales trainers, they will make dumb comments about some random object in their prospect's office as if that is enough to initiate a relationship. Far too many sales people just go through the motions to check Build Rapport off their sales-process list so they can get down to selling.

Buyers are not fooled. They find these lame attempts at rapport building gratuitous and insincere. Over time, they become numb to rapport-building efforts. Some think it is funny. I have a friend who is a buyer for a manufacturing company. He has the ugliest picture in his office you have ever seen. He keeps it there for one reason: to watch salespeople humiliate themselves by asking him questions about the picture in an attempt to build rapport. If you want people to buy you, forget about rapport. Remove the word from your vocabulary. Instead, focus on *connecting*.

The Real Secret to Connecting

There is a quote from Abraham Lincoln that aptly sums up why rapport as a strategy fails. Lincoln said, *"If you would win a man to your cause, first convince him that you are his sincere friend."* Rapport is designed not to develop trusting relationships, but rather to influence behavior. Rapport in its purest form is manipulative.

People who feel manipulated will be distrustful of your motivations, no matter how pure, and will never feel connected to you. Connecting, on the other hand, is designed to win others over through a focus on them. The most effective strategy for winning others over (convincing them that you are their friend) is to start and end by helping them get what they want.

The most insatiable human desire, our deepest craving, is to feel valued, appreciated, and important. The key to connecting and winning others over is, therefore, extremely simple: *make them feel important*. The real secret to making others feel important is something you have at your disposal right now. *It's listening*. Listening is powerful. Listening is exactly why Jennifer, from the opening story, walked out of that dealership a winner. Quite simply, the more you listen, the more connected others will feel to you. When you listen, you make people feel important, valued, and appreciated.

Unfortunately, no one is really listening. I realize this is a harsh and general indictment of virtually everyone, but it is true. Why? Because we would rather think about and talk about ourselves, our wants and needs, our accomplishments, and our problems. This is easy to observe. Just go to a networking event, business meeting, or sales call. If people aren't talking over each other in their eagerness to express their own self-important point of view, they are waiting impatiently for the other person to stop talking so they can start. The vast majority of people, especially salespeople, never make the effort to sincerely listen to others. They don't like to listen because listening doesn't make them feel important. Much of the time when they are not talking they are thinking about what they are going to say next. Trust me; you are your own favorite person. It is not your fault; it is part of being human, but it is a roadblock to building connections with others—especially in business.

There is real power in understanding this concept and using it to your advantage to build connections. The desire to feel important, valued, and appreciated is more insatiable than any other human craving. Just like you, when people talk about themselves and someone listens, it makes them feel important. Although truly listening to another person requires self-discipline, selflessness, practice, and patience, it is not complicated or complex. That is the beauty of connecting. Unlike the complexity of rapport, connecting requires only that you listen to your prospect, customer, client, boss, or peer.

Ask Questions

Thomas Freese, author of *Question Based Selling*, teaches that "a question you ask is more important than anything you will ever say." Questions start conversations, reveal problems, and demonstrate that you are paying attention and listening. Questions are critical to connecting because with questions you give the other person the opportunity to talk. In the next chapter you will learn how to use questions to uncover problems. In this section you will learn how to use questions to connect.

Ask Easy Questions

With ongoing relationships, questions can be as simple as, "Hey, John, how's your family?" Because you know each other and have already established a relationship, there will be easy entry points. But what about the first time you are meeting your prospect or perhaps someone at a networking event? How should you get the conversation started? Imagine that a stranger walks up to you on the street and starts asking you personal questions. How would it feel? What would you say? How quickly would you put your emotional wall up, attempt to disengage, and run the other way? Imagine how a prospect feels the first time she meets a salesperson. She knows the salesperson's motivation is, first and foremost, to sell her something. Because of this, she is mentally prepared to keep rapport building at arm's length to avoid being manipulated. The salesperson walks into her office and begins peppering her with personal and business questions designed to build rapport. It is human nature to put up an emotional wall when strangers start asking hard questions, and our buyer has her's firmly in place. With the wall up, the conversation quickly stalls. The salesperson reverts to what is most comfortable, begins talking about himself, and then starts pitching his product. The net result is no connection, no problem solving, and no sale.

The key to breaking through this wall is starting conversations with questions that are easy for your prospect to answer and that your prospect will enjoy answering. When they start talking, give them your complete attention. That is most critical. When people get your undivided attention it makes them feel good. This reinforces answering your questions with a positive reward (a behavior that receives a positive reward tends to repeat itself), which causes your prospect to want to answer more of your questions, further pulling the wall down. The more closely you pay attention to the other person and become genuinely interested in what they are saying, the more valuable and important they will feel. The better they feel, the more they will want to talk. The more they talk, the more connected they will feel to you. As you connect, the wall will continue to come down until you gain the right to ask the deeper, more strategic questions that will eventually help you uncover their problems.

What are easy questions? They are questions that are not too personal or probing but that, at the same time, gives the other person something real to talk about. Note that the question must be sincere. Asking a cheesy question about some random object on their desk is useless. It does not come across as sincere or leave room for you to ask follow up questions that will keep the conversation moving and the wall coming down. One of my favorite easy questions when I'm meeting with a potential client for the first time is, "How long have you been working here?" If they say 20 years, it gives me the opportunity to acknowledge the accomplishment (which gives them approval and makes them feel valued). Then I follow up with, "I bet you've seen a lot of changes around here!" and with that the floodgate usually opens. On the other hand, if they say six months I can ask, "What made you decide to work here?" In this case I learn about their motivations, career aspirations, and background. This opens up the opportunity for a wide array of follow-up questions, which again makes my prospect feel important, keeps them talking, and pulls their emotional wall down.

Common ground is another source of easy questions. If your prospect reveals something you both have in common—you went to the same school, live in the same neighborhood, know the same people, have the same hobby, and so forth—you'll have a natural jumping off point for easy questions. The pitfall with common ground is it can be so familiar and comfortable that instead of allowing your prospect to talk, you take over the conversation. When you begin pontificating on the subject with the illusion that your prospect will perceive you as knowledgeable, your connection is broken. Trust me, people don't want to listen to you talk, they want to listen to themselves talk. When discussing a subject that you have in common with your prospect, try not to use statements to demonstrate your knowledge of the subject. Instead, ask your prospect intelligent questions related to the subject so they do the talking. Never forget that a question is far more important than anything you say.

Be Prepared

Technology and the Internet have made gathering information about others as simple as a few key strokes on Google. When you are afforded the opportunity, prepare in advance of your meeting by researching the person you are meeting with. Look for accomplishments or events that they will be proud to talk about but that are not too personal or deep. When you ask about achievements, you give the other person something easy to talk about while making them feel important. You demonstrate that you care and are paying attention to them, which makes them feel appreciated and valued. All people have a deep need for approval of their actions and accomplishments. This need is ongoing and is never satisfied for long. When you praise the accomplishments of others, you build their self-esteem. Bestselling author and speaker Brian Tracy says "People who continually seek opportunities

to express approval are welcome wherever they go."
With a little effort, you can develop a set of easy questions that are appropriate in various situation and that
are designed to get others to start talking.

Listening

Have you ever noticed how often you have a conversation with your spouse, friends, children, boss,
prospects, or customers, and shortly afterward, one or
both of you disagree about what was said or agreed to?
If you really think about it, this happens often. How is
it possible? You were both there, either on the phone
or staring at each other face-to-face, and you each
walked away with a different understanding of what
happened?

Almost every book on sales, in one form or
another, admonishes that listening is the key to real success. In sales and leadership trainings, business professionals are taught communication and listening skills.
There are thousands of seminars, books, and audio
programs dedicated to communication and listening
(a Google search yielded 13 million results for listening skills and more than 10,000 books about listening
listed on Amazon). Yet, time and again, in conversation after conversation, messages get scrambled and
there is disagreement. One party or the other wonders
aloud, "Why doesn't anybody listen?"

Back when I was in fourth grade, my teacher, Ms. Gibbons, took the entire class outside on a warm spring day. She lined us all up, about 25 kids, and on one end of the line whispered a message that she read from an index card into the ear of the first child in line. That child then turned to the next person in line and whispered the same message. The process continued as each fourth grader whispered the message to the next in line until we reached the end. Ms Gibbons then had the last child repeat the message out loud to all of the other children. There were giggles and snickers. We were all shaking our heads. The words that came out of the last child's mouth were not the words we had passed on. Finally, Ms. Gibbons read from the index card. The words she spoke were foreign to almost everyone except the first few people in line. Over the course of 25 repetitions, the message had been so convoluted that it no longer resembled the original. I can clearly remember how shocked I was. The demonstration of how poorly we listen was so powerful it has stuck with me for the last 40 years. I think about it each time there is a breakdown in communication, which is actually a breakdown in listening.

Despite all that we have been taught and all that we know, listening is still the weakest link in human interaction. Of course it is likely that you already know this because you are interacting with people and they are not listening to you. It is likely that you have thrown your hands up in disgust and said "Why won't these people listen to me?" or "What do I need to do to get my message through to them?" or "My kids (*husband, wife, friends, employees*) just don't hear what I'm saying!" It is frustrating and it makes you feel unappreciated and undervalued. It hurts your connections. If there is any good news, it is that you are not alone. It turns out that feeling this way is the human condition. It seems nobody is listening to anybody. Everyone is frustrated. We all want to be heard. We scream out silently from the inside, "Will somebody just listen to me!"

The question is, "Why does this happen and what can we do about it?" The answer is as simple as it is complex. The reason we don't listen is that listening requires effort and focus whereas *not listening* is easy. It is hard to tune out all of the distracting noise; it is hard to be patient and wait our turn; it is hard not to look down at our BlackBerry or at our computer screen or the TV; and it is very, very hard to turn off our own thoughts long enough to really pay attention to another person.

On the other hand, it is so much easier to talk. Talking makes us feel important. It is so easy, in fact, that talking instead of listening is an ingrained bad habit for most people. The fact is that we spend about 95 percent of our time thinking (or talking) about ourselves and listening to our own thoughts. The other 5 percent of the time we are trying to get rid of problems so that we can go back to thinking about ourselves.

So how to change this terrible habit that inhibits your ability to connect and solve problems? Read books about listening skills? Go to listening training? Nope! The answer is simple: pay attention to the other person. Amazing, isn't it? If you want to listen better, give the other person your undivided attention. In other words, *be there*. Just become genuinely interested in the other person and hear what they are saying with all of your senses.

Sounds simple, right? Well, not exactly. It is easy for me to say "give others your undivided attention" but it is very hard to actually do it. You have developed the habit of being self-absorbed over the course of a lifetime. To turn everything in your head off, become genuinely interested in another person, give them your undivided attention, and *really* hear them will be the hardest habit you will ever break. It will require faith that really listening will improve your relationships, income, and career. You have to believe that when you listen you will build stronger connections. You'll also have to overcome the instinct to talk and recognize that you talk because it makes you feel important.

When you make the commitment to give others your complete attention and really listen, your career will prosper and your sales will soar. You will know exactly what your customers really want. When you take time to concentrate, turn off your own thoughts, and really pay attention to another person, you will quickly find that people are willing to do anything for you.

The Art of Listening

Almost everyone in business has attended at least one training session during which they were taught a module on active listening. Active listening is essentially a set of behaviors that are designed to demonstrate to the other person that you are listening. We've already established that the fastest and most effective way to connect with another person is to listen to them, because listening makes them feel important. If you want to make them feel unimportant and lose that connection, all you need to do is leave them with the perception that you are not listening. With this in mind, active listening behaviors will serve you well.

Active listening behaviors include making eye contact, acknowledging with verbal feedback and body language, summarizing and restating what you have heard, and utilizing pauses and silence before speaking. The misconception about active listening is that by practicing these behaviors you will actually *be* listening. It is completely possible to go through the motions of active listening yet not really hear a thing. Note, though, that acting like you are listening is far better than having the other person feel that you are not listening. At least they walk away from the meeting feeling valued and that you care. Turning listening into a connection that leads to problem solving, and then into a long-term relationship, however, requires you to actually listen. This means that, in addition to demonstrating that you are listening with active listening behaviors, you also have to remove all other distractions including your own self-centered thoughts and give the other person your complete attention.

Focusing completely on the person in front of you and being genuinely interested in what they are saying is a learned behavior. Before each meeting, make a commitment to yourself to turn off your own thoughts, desires, and impatience and place all your attention on the other person. You may even have to say it out loud and prepare yourself mentally to remain focused on the other person. Be aware of your urge to blurt out your idea or tune the other person out when you find them boring. Once you are aware of these behaviors it will be much easier to self-correct. After each conversation, evaluate how well you paid attention, acknowledge your shortcomings, and renew your commitment. When you do this consistently, you will find that listening becomes easier. One thing to remember over the course of your career is that *people never complain about people who listen.*

Eye Contact

Remember Jim Rohn's quote from the last chapter, "Wherever you are, be there?" This concept is as apropos for listening as it is for likability. Controlling your self-centered thoughts is the key to being there mentally. Controlling your eyes keeps you there physically. Wherever you point your eyes is what you will concentrate on. Practice maintaining good eye contact at all times. Whether face to face or on the phone, avoid the burning desire to multitask by keeping your eyes off papers, computer screens, cell phones, BlackBerries, and TVs. Turn your electronics off so that beeps, dings, and buzzes don't cause you to look away. The moment you make the mistake of looking away, you'll not only lose concentration, but you will offend the other person. One trick is to look at the other person's eyes and make a note of their eye color. When you do this it forces you to make solid and genuine eye contact in the critical, first few seconds of a conversation.

Listen Deeply

Eye contact, though central to listening, only plays a part. Author Tim Sanders coined the term "listening deeply" to describe listening as an eyes, ears, and emotional experience. In other words, watch the speaker's body language and expression; analyze the tone, timbre, and pace of the speaker's voice; hear the words; and step into the speaker's shoes empathically. Since people communicate with far more than words, opening up your other senses affords you the opportunity to analyze the emotional nuances of the conversation. Listening deeply shows the other person that you get them and naturally draws you closer and strengthens your connection.

When you listen deeply, you are looking for emotional cues, verbal and nonverbal, that open the door to relevant follow-up questions that lubricate the conversation by keeping the other person talking about things that interest him or her. It is easy to keep people engaged when they are talking about themselves. Follow-up questions also allow you to employ the active listening behaviors of summarizing and restating, which show that you are listening, without making statements. Unlike statements that tend to stall conversations, questions keep them flowing. Questions also slow down the pace and allow you to clarify your understanding, which is very important for uncovering problems. Never forget, the more the other person is talking, the more connected they feel to you.

Keep Them Talking

There are other active listening behaviors that help you keep conversations moving. Supporting phrases like "yes, I see," "I understand," and "that's exciting" keep the other person talking and show that you are listening. In the same vein, behaviors like nodding your head and smiling in approval and leaning forward when you find something they say particularly interesting keep them talking and show that you are listening. One sure way to kill a conversation is to blurt out your next question or statement or, worse, talk over the speaker before they have finished speaking. This makes it transparent that you are not listening, but rather formulating the next thing you plan to say. When you think the other person has finished speaking, pause and count to two before speaking again. This affords you time to fully digest what you have heard before responding. Most importantly, it leaves room for the other person to finish speaking and prevents you from cutting them off if they have not.

The bottom line is that listening requires that you give your attention to the other person. To do so, you will have to develop the discipline to turn off your natural inclination to focus on your thoughts and put aside your desire to talk to satisfy your own need to feel important. Listening requires you to have faith that when you are listening you are in control and by listening you connect and win others over. It takes practice to really listen, and you will make many mistakes along the way. However, when you develop the habit of listening, your network and friendships will grow and your likability, reputation, income, and career will soar.

Staying Connected

The longer you maintain a relationship, the more connected you will be to your client. You will find it easier to initiate and engage in conversations, and those conversations will be more comfortable and revealing. However, nurturing connections requires vigilance. No matter how long you have known the other person or how comfortable you feel with them, you must always remember to give them your complete attention and listen. Make an effort to avoid talking about yourself and focus on making them feel appreciated and important. Seek out opportunities to compliment and praise their accomplishments. Learn and remember the names of their spouses and children and make note of and acknowledge special days like birthdays, anniversaries, graduations, weddings, and other events that are important to them. Doing so demonstrates with tangible evidence that you are genuinely interested in them and their needs, and that you value and appreciate them.

Remember and Use Names

Remembering and using names when you greet others and in conversations plays an important role in maintaining connections. The one word we respond to and long to hear above all others is our own name. When

we are called by name, we feel valued and acknowledged. It sounds beautiful to us. When you remember
and use the names of secretaries, security guards, influencers, and others in your customers' accounts, you
instantly win them to your cause. Forget about the
old excuse, "I'm terrible with names." You cannot afford the luxury of this excuse. Failing to remember
names or mispronouncing names diminishes your likability, breaks connections, and harms your reputation.
Frankly, most people don't remember names because
remembering names requires work. It is easier to be
lazy. Being terrible with names is a choice. *Choose* to
develop a system to remember names. You'll find thousands of worthwhile articles and videos with tips on
how to remember names with just a quick search on
Google. Taking time to read these articles and review
the tips is worthwhile. You will find, though, that the
common threads running across all these resources are
the following tips:

- **Commitment:** Deciding and remaining committed to have the self-discipline to remember
  names. (This is not much different than making the commitment to listen.) Commitment is
  a choice only you can make.
- **Concentration:** Paying attention when someone says his or her name. This means really listening to the name and how it is pronounced. In
  other words, you have to be there. If you miss the

name, don't let the moment pass without asking the person to tell it to you again.

- **Repetition:** Repeating the name to yourself until you seal it into your memory.
- **Association:** Associating the name with something else that is easier to remember. A place, company, sound, idea, visual cue, and so forth.

I have a good friend who seems to have the uncanny ability to remember the name of every person he has ever met. At first glance, it appears to be some sort of magic. On closer observation, though, his secret is revealed. The technique he uses, not just for names, but also for remembering events and subjects of conversations, is to immediately make a note of important things to remember and associate with the person he met. He just makes his notes right on the back of their business card. He then enters this information, without fail, in greater detail into his customer relationship management (CRM) program at the close of each day before his memory fades. Then, he reviews the information again the following morning to ensure he has remembered the name and associated it to the person. He has more friends than anyone I know.

Remembering and using names is a win–win way to initiate and maintain connections. It will make you more likable, burnish your reputation, and make it easy for people to buy you.

Sales Tip: Staying Connected with E-Mail and Voice Mail

A surefire way to damage your connections and relationships is with poor voice mail, e-mail, and text message etiquette. With these communication tools it is not so much what you say but how you say it. It is easy to injure others with an offensive, demanding, or overpowering tone of voice or written word. It happens daily. The nicest, most polite people cause great offense with a simple e-mail message. Making things worse is the fact that e-mails, text messages, and voice mails that others find offensive can be easily forwarded, which further harms your reputation and fuels the fire.

Sometimes a simple message (mostly e-mail messages) is the spark that ignites a war that damages connections and relationships beyond repair in the blink of an eye. It all starts out innocently enough. One party sends a message to another in the attempt to communicate a frustration, concern, want, or need. The receiving party reads the message and becomes offended by the tone. That party then fires back a response (without thinking), which offends the original sender. This exchange of fire continues until both parties, exasperated, are so angry that not only does the original issue go unresolved, but they are often unable to work amicably with each other again. The biggest fights and relationship disintegrations I have witnessed in recent years have been the result of e-mail exchanges.

The major problem with e-mail and text messages is the other person can't see or hear you. Interpersonal communication is a combination of words, voice tone, timbre and inflection, body language, and facial expression. When others are unable to associate the words they are reading with the context of your voice tone and facial expressions, they assign their own meaning to the emotions they read into the words. This is why there is rampant miscommunication with e-mail, text messaging, and, at a growing level, with social-networking tools.

Voice mail is different in that you have the opportunity to communicate through words and voice tone, timbre, and inflection. The problem with voice mail is the other person isn't on the other end of the line to react to your tone of voice with their own verbal cues or to clarify your meaning in the event that they misunderstand your tone. The other problem with voice mail is that if the receiving party does take offense they can play your voice mail over and over, which only serves to rub salt in the wound. Although far less dangerous than e-mail, many salespeople, in particular, injure relationships through voice mail. This is done most often when they express frustration or exasperation when a deal is stalled, when they are missing information or

(continued)

(*Continued*)

action items from support staff, or when they are not getting call backs. (Managers run into similar problems when leaving stern or demanding voices mails for their subordinates.) Voice mail makes it easy to vent with negative emotion, which can and will come back to bite you.

These communication tools, while important and useful, are extremely dangerous to connections and relationships. They can, however, be managed to your advantage by following some simple rules:

- Never express negative emotions: Never express negative emotions like frustration, anger, disappointment, exasperation, or sarcasm. Never criticize—even if the other person has asked for your critique. Negative emotions and criticisms should only be dealt with live, either on the phone or in person.
- Express positive emotions: E-mail, voice mail, and text messaging are fantastic tools for praising, complimenting, and expressing gratitude to others. With these tools you can instantly make someone feel valued, important, and appreciated—an excellent way to strengthen connections. What's more, they can send your message to others (which makes them feel even more important), and listen to or read it time and again.

- Just give the facts: Messaging tools are perfect for conveying facts and arranging meetings. Used in this manner, they become assets that allow you to get more done in less time.

- Pause before pushing Send: Once you push Send you cannot get your message back. Few of us have not experienced regret over a message we sent in haste. Develop the discipline to pause before hitting Send (this is especially important if you are on the receiving end of a message that angered you and you are about to fire back a response). Before you send a message, check the tone to ensure that you are expressing either positive emotions or facts. Proofread your e-mails and text messages, and play your voice mails back to be sure your message is professional and easy to understand. Stand in the receiver's shoes and consider how you would feel if you were on the receiving end of the message. NEVER, ever, ever send a message when you are angry or frustrated. When in this state, resist the temptation to send a message, and decide instead to come back to it at another time. You'll be amazed at how different things look when you pause.

- When in doubt, pick up the phone: The most effective way to communicate is in real time. No

(*continued*)

(*Continued*)

matter how brilliant you believe your communication skills to be, you cannot win an argument or carry on a conversation via e-mail. You will always do more harm than good attempting to clarify misunderstandings with messaging tools. When you sense frustration, need to convey negative emotion or criticism, or are looking for clarification, pick up the phone and make a call. In virtually all cases, a short phone call clears things up and leaves both parties feeling heard, appreciated, and understood. If you want to use messaging tools to your advantage, practice this rule before pushing Send. If there is even a slight bit of doubt about how your message will be received and interpreted, pick up the phone.

Summary

Connecting opens the door to problem solving. Unlike rapport building, which is a convoluted approach to influencing behavior, connecting is about building an emotional bond with another person so that they feel comfortable discussing their real problems with you. You connect by giving others what they want the most—feeling appreciated, valued, and important. Listening is the real secret to connecting. The fastest and most effective way to make others feel important

is to give them an opportunity to talk about themselves. To listen effectively you learn to be genuinely
interested in and give others your complete attention.
The more people talk, the closer they will feel to
you and the more comfortable they will feel revealing
their true problems, which, when solved, will create a
profitable and loyal business relationship.

5 | Solve Problems

I waited patiently in the lobby of a major food-processing and distribution company. It was the largest account in my territory. Because of an expiring contract with my competitor, the buying window was open. Finally Sam, the Purchasing Manager, came out to get me. He apologized for being late and offered me a seat in his office. I got right down to business. I told him about my company and why I thought we were a good fit for his company. Sam gave me an overview of his situation and said, "We are ending our relationship with your competitor and we are ready to move forward. I want to make a decision next week. How soon do you think I can get a proposal?"

I quickly set an appointment to bring back a proposal the next week. As I walked to the parking lot, I was elated. It looked like this account would be mine. Back at the office, I put together a beautiful PowerPoint presentation using my best slides and graphics. I assembled product samples and gathered my top food industry references. My pricing was competitive, and I was sure it would get Sam's attention.

On the morning of my presentation to Sam I put on my best suit and tie and walked confidently to my car, ready to close the deal. Since I had only been with the company for six months I brought my sales manager, Bob, along for support. Sam met us in the lobby, and ushered us into a conference room. Then nervously looking at his watch, he said he'd give us time to set up and left the room.

A few minutes later Sam walked into the conference room followed by an older gentleman. He introduced us to Ken, the president of the company. I handed them each a copy of the proposal and began the presentation. About five minutes in I noticed, out of the corner of my eye, that Bob was squirming in his seat. Then suddenly and loudly Bob said, "Jeb, stop!" I had already been nervous because Ken had joined the meeting and now my face flushed red with heat and my knees buckled. Before I could respond, Bob looked across the table and said "Ken, I'm sensing that you aren't exactly impressed by our presentation."

The company president was sitting back in his chair with his arms crossed. The expression on his face said it all. My presentation turned into a train wreck. Ken looked directly at Bob and said, "You're damn right I'm not impressed. This is the same crap all of you guys bring in here. We've changed vendors four times in the last ten years and it's always for the same reasons.

I just don't understand why you folks can't get it right. This is the third presentation I've seen this week, and it looks exactly like the other ones. I'm beginning to wonder if, to save money, you and your competitors have all hired the same marketing company."

Ken was pounding on the table, "I've heard the same promises over and over again. But you know what, last week your competitor shut down our line. Do you know what happens when our line gets shut down? We go out of business! We had to send every one of our employees home last Friday. So, I'm sorry to tell you this, but I don't believe you and I don't believe your promises. You are all the same and I am sick and tired of listening to this."

It was then that my six-foot-three sales manager stood up, reached over to Ken's side of the conference table and grabbed the proposal. Then, with every ounce of energy he could muster, he slammed it on the floor. It sounded like a gun had fired! I looked over at Sam. His eyes were as big around as dinner plates. Then there was dead silence. I wanted to crawl under the table. Bob slowly turned back toward Ken. He leaned forward, looked the company president square in the eyes and said, "You're right. We are all the same, but we don't have to be."

Bob was in the zone. He slipped off his jacket, unbuttoned his cuffs and rolled up his sleeves. He looked at Ken and then over at Sam and matter-of-factly said, "Let's get to work. Tell me something, if you could design the perfect program for your company, what would it look like?" Ken leaned in, his demeanor completely changed. He was all business, but there was a smile on his face as he opened up and told us exactly what he wanted. I scribbled notes as fast as I could while Bob asked follow-up questions.

Ken took us to meet with each department head, and we asked more questions. An hour later we sat back down in the conference room and wrapped things up. Bob said, "Here is what it sounds like we need to do to solve your problems once and for all." Then he reviewed what we had learned. "Are we on the right track?" They said yes. Bob then looked at Ken and said, "If we can do this will we get your business?"

"Absolutely," Ken replied.

We came back a week later with a plan that solved their problems for good. Ken signed without hesitation, even though it was a 40 percent premium over what he had been paying our competitor. For me it was the lesson of a lifetime. Walking out of the previous appointment I was as embarrassed as I had ever been. My presentation had been a complete crash and burn in front of my sales manager. I'd screwed up badly by taking shortcuts. I had never connected with Sam and did not take the time to ask questions. I just *assumed* that I knew what they needed. Bob pointed out how lucky I'd been that Ken had come to the meeting with Sam. Otherwise, I would have lost the account and never known why. Following Bob around that plant and listening to him ask questions was a real eye opener. The biggest lesson I learned was that, when you ask questions you find problems, and when you solve problems you close business. Almost 20 years later, I still have the letter Ken sent us thanking us for doing what none of our competitors had been able to do. In the last line of the letter he wrote, "I've learned that you are not all the same."

The Problem with Pump and Dump

On a recent business trip, while sitting at the hotel bar, I met a corporate buyer who was in town for a seminar. After some small talk I asked him what he thought of the sales profession in general. His response was not at all what I was expecting. He just looked down at his drink and matter-of-factly said, "Salespeople bore me." His comment caught me so off guard that at first I was speechless. I replied, "That wasn't exactly what I was expecting you would say. Could you tell me what you mean?"

He said, "Look, I get paid to talk to salespeople and that is what I do all day. Now, there are some salespeople who I really like working with, but the vast majority bore me to death. They come in, sit down, insincerely ask me how I'm doing, make a comment about something in my office, ask a handful of generic questions, pitch their company or product, ask me to give them my business, and are usually flabbergasted when I don't. It's like they are all cut from the same mold."

The salespeople who walked into his office failed because they pumped and dumped. Sales expert and author Kelly Robertson says, "It may sound simple, but most sales people don't get it. They still believe that selling means talking at great length about their company, their product, or their service. However, truly effective selling is all about asking the prospect the right questions and demonstrating that you can help them solve a particular problem or issue. That means you need to direct *all* your attention to their situation and resist the opportunity to talk about your company or your offering."

Intuitively, most salespeople know that they should show interest in their prospects. But frankly, it is easier to give a dissertation than to ask questions and be attentive and interested Since it is human nature to take the easy way out, this is what most salespeople do. Think about what it feels like to be on the other end of a conversation in which someone is just talking about herself—it is boring. That is how buyers feel when salespeople pitch or dump instead of asking questions.

The Conflict of Objectives

Solving problems is the foundation of the *People Buy You* philosophy. Solving problems is about helping other people get what they want. When you help others get what they want, you will get what you want. For example, when you help your client solve a business problem with your product or service, you get a commission check.

Once you become comfortable with the *People Buy You* levers, you will find that others are drawn to you and you will have little problem engaging them in conversations. In personal relationships, having long conversations about whatever subject comes to mind is no big deal. However, in business relationships, the reason you are in the conversation in the first place is *business*.

The difference between business conversations and personal conversations is that business conversations have an objective. In other words, at least one of the parties has a strategic or tactical objective for the meeting, and both parties, at least tacitly, believe there is some reasonable value in meeting with the other party. As a sales and business professional, you should never enter into a business conversation, whether with a prospect, customer, manager, support staff, or peer without a clear objective for the outcome of that meeting.

The conflict you face is people buy (or take action) for their reasons, not yours. Though you may have an objective for the meeting (close the sale), unless your prospect clearly gets a benefit that meets his or her objective (solve my problem), you will not achieve your objective. This is where so many salespeople fail, and this is why the buyer I met complained that "salespeople bore him." People are interested in what they want, not what you want. They want their problems solved. When you lead with a pitch for your product, service, idea, or desire, you are speaking in your language, not in theirs.

Five Rules of Questioning

When it comes to problem solving, questions are king. Learning and practicing effective questioning skills are central to a successful career in sales and business. Before we dive deeper into questioning strategies, I want to explain five rules of questioning. These rules will guide you in asking the right questions, at the right time, in the right way.

Rule 1: People Won't Tell You Their Real Problems until They Feel Connected to You

We covered this extensively in Chapter 4. When you first meet people, they have their wall up. Connecting is designed to pull the wall down. You connect by listening, giving people your complete attention, and being genuinely interested in what they have to say.

Rule 2: Ask Easy Questions First

To get people to reveal their problems, you need them
to talk. The more they talk, the more problems they
will reveal. To make it easy for people to talk, start the
conversation off with questions that are easy for your
prospect to answer and that they will enjoy answering.
Once they feel comfortable talking, you can begin
asking deeper, more strategic questions that will reveal
their real problems.

Rule 3: People Communicate with Stories

In conversations, people don't spit out facts. Instead,
they use stories. When you listen attentively, you encourage the speaker to expand on and tell more stories.
The clues that lead to their real problems are buried
inside these stories.

Rule 4: Be Empathetic—Follow Emotional Cues to Problems

Listening deeply with your eyes, ears, and heart will
lead you to emotional cues like voice inflection, facial
expressions, and body language, which indicate that a
story point or issue has emotional significance. When

you find these cues, use follow-up questions to dig deeper. This is where real problems will be revealed.

Rule 5: Never Make Assumptions

Many salespeople assume that they know exactly what their prospect needs. After a little rapport building, they move right into their scripted pitch. They dump features and benefits and explain how their product or service is the perfect match. They assume, rather than ask questions, because they are in a hurry, bored, impatient, or lack empathy. Besides all of the obvious pitfalls of assuming, there is also an emotional trap. No one—not you, not me, not your prospects—likes to be told that he or she is not unique. We resent it. We want to be treated as individuals. The key is to get your prospects talking about what they want and need, no matter how obvious the problem.

Empathy and Problem Solving

In author Dean Koontz's words, "Some people think only intellect counts: knowing how to solve problems, knowing how to get by, knowing how to identify an advantage and seize it. But the functions of intellect are insufficient without . . . empathy." Business requires intellect and empathy. Both play vital roles in relationships, communication, and problem solving. Empathy is the ability to step into someone else's shoes and see things from their perspective. It is the ability to understand and identify with another's feelings or motives. Empathy comes easy when you give others your complete attention, listen deeply, turn off your thoughts, and become genuinely interested in what they are saying.

Empathy gives you insight into the perspective of the speaker and helps you overcome the habit of assuming you know what is best for him. It helps you see each person as a unique individual. This is when you understand that regardless of how common a problem may be, each person views her own problems as special. When you stand in another person's shoes and see problems from that person's perspective, you may then tap into your intellect to deliver personalized solutions that validates to that person that you view him or her as unique. These personalized solutions are the key to closing business, building trust, and customer retention.

Look Out for Icebergs

If you've ever had a chance to see an iceberg up close, you know how impressively huge they can be. What is hard to fathom, though, is that the tip of the iceberg is only a small portion of the total mass, which is hidden below the surface. Those who navigate the oceans recognize that it is this hidden mass that poses the greatest danger to their vessels. On ships that sail in seas where icebergs float, there is always someone on lookout. Failure to heed the danger posed by the hidden mass of icebergs leads to disastrous and fatal consequences.

In sales, our customers and prospects are just like icebergs, often revealing to us just a fraction of the information we need, while their real problems are hidden from view. Until you get beneath the surface, you have no way of knowing if you are addressing the most important issues for your client.

Consider Joe, an account executive, who walks into the office of a new prospect, introduces himself, and begins pitching his company and products. After his initial pitch, he (as taught in his company's sales training) transitions into asking questions like: "How is your current vendor doing?" "Are you happy?" "What don't you like about your current program, product, service?" "How much do you order each week, month, year?"

Linda, the buyer, plays her role perfectly (just as she was taught in buyer's school) and responds to each of Joe's questions. With the questioning part of the sales call checked off, Joe presents the features and benefits of his product and makes his proposal. Comfortable that he has moved through the sales process flawlessly, Joe goes for the close, "Linda, it looks like we can save you money. We can have your first order delivered next week. All you need to do is sign here." Linda politely explains to Joe that she needs more time to work down her existing inventory. If he'll sharpen his pencil, he can call back in two weeks and she will be ready to place an order. Joe walks out to his car, calls his sales manager, says he had a good meeting, and that the deal is in the bag.

Two weeks later, Joe, anticipating an easy close, calls Linda back. After a quick exchange of pleasantries, Linda explains that she's decided to go with one of Joe's competitors for her widgets instead. Stunned, Joe asks why. Linda explains that the other vendor had a better solution to her most pressing problem—*a problem that Joe knew nothing about.* Joe stammers back, "You didn't say anything about that issue. I wish I had known. We have the best solution on the market for that problem. Will you please reconsider? I can be back over there in an hour!" But, alas, it is too late. The decision has been made. Joe's ship is sunk. Why didn't Joe know about this problem? During his questioning he never got below the surface. And unfortunately it is not in the nature of buyers to show sellers the problems below the surface. *Look out for icebergs, Joe!*

Joe is a *pump and dump* salesperson. He pumped Linda for basic information and then dumped his features and benefits in her lap. If Joe had read *People Buy You,* he would have connected first and then used that connection to ask deeper, more strategic questions to get below the surface. Instead of focusing on his features and benefits, he would have learned about Linda's problems.

The Transition from Connecting to Problem Solving

As you move from *connecting* to *problem solving,* resist the temptation to pitch your product or service. Dumping product or company information on your prospect or customer at this point will break the connection you established. Maintain your connection by focusing acute attention on the other person and keep them talking by asking easy questions. These kind of questions help you make the transition into a business conversation centered around problem solving. My favorite easy questions are "do" questions.

- "I've done some research on your company. Can you tell me more about what you do here?"
- "How do you do that?"
- "Where do you (produce, service, manufacture, ship) this?"
- "What else do you do here?
- "Can you tell me more about what that new product you are manufacturing does?"

These questions let the other person talk about things that are familiar. Since people tend to communicate in stories, listen deeply to pick up unsaid feelings and emotions. Watch for facial expressions, body language, and voice tonality that offer clues to underlying importance. You don't have to be an expert in body language to see obvious clues. You only need to be observant and prepared to ask follow-up questions to test your hunch, like "That sounds pretty important. How are you dealing with it?"

Listening and asking follow-up questions this way has two benefits. It makes the other person feel important and creates a deeper feeling of connection, and it opens access to the emotions and problems that lie below the surface. It is at this point that your questions may become more focused, specific, and relevant to your overriding business objective. You will be able to engage the other person to reveal their problems.

It is the ability to be intellectual while remaining empathetic that makes you a superstar. This dual-process questioning (maintaining focus on your strategic objectives while engaging your prospect emotionally) is the key to getting below the surface and identifying *real* problems.

Most salespeople use a linear questioning process. They go through a checklist of questions that help them gather just enough information to present a proposal to their prospect. There is no connection, only a simple conveyance of facts. Dual-process questioning is nonlinear in nature. It is designed to be fluid, flexible, and open to multiple avenues of questioning that access the buyer's emotions and provide a clearer picture of the problems, pitfalls, and issues that lie below the surface.

When you connect with your buyer emotionally, by demonstrating empathy, the door will be opened for you to ask in-depth questions. Using the fluid, dual-process questioning allows you the flexibility to adjust your questions strategically as you uncover the problems that are most emotional and pressing to your buyer. It is then that you gain the insight to build a bridge that links your buyer's problems to your organization's solutions.

About Questions

Here is a fact: the more questions you ask, the more sales you will close. To solve a problem, you must first uncover the problem. To do that, you ask questions. The reason I continue to repeat this mantra is that most salespeople and business professionals don't ask enough questions.

You've likely been through some type of training program in which you were taught about open-ended and closed-ended questions. In the training you learned that open-ended questions are good and closed-ended questions are bad. From there, a few general examples of open-ended questions and closed-ended questions were passed around the training room and, unfortunately, the questioning module was then concluded.

These training programs are effective in teaching you the difference between open- and closed-ended questions, but ineffective in teaching how to apply questioning skills in the real world. If you were to interview 100 sales professionals, 99 of them would tell you that open-ended questions are the most important questions in sales. However, if you were to observe these same salespeople interacting with customers and prospects, you would mostly hear closed-ended questions and features and benefits dumps.

To be effective at questioning, you have got to be able to ask questions as smoothly as an actor delivers lines in a scene of a play. Your questions have to be scripted and practiced so that they sound natural. Questions also have to be engrained in your memory so that you can access them in a nonlinear way, based on the specific situation and client.

You need to develop regular "go-to" questions, including easy questions for getting conversations started, clarifying questions for checking emotional cues, and general questions like "worry" questions. Worry questions are excellent tools for getting others to open up to you about their problems. Worry questions will not work unless you have established a connection. My favorite worry question is, "When you lay your head on your pillow at night and think about this 'situation,' what do you worry about?" "What worries you about that 'situation'?" and "What concerns you the most about this 'situation'?" are other variations. The worry question is a great go-to question, because it is easy to remember. When you ask it, you are guaranteed to get a story that will reveal emotional hot buttons. There are many resources available that offer lists of general sales questions. My recommendation is that you review these lists and adopt (or alter) the questions that feel most comfortable to you. That way, when you ask the questions, you will sound natural.

In addition to go-to questions, you also need an inventory of questions that are specifically relevant to your product, service, or management situation. Unfortunately, most training programs are not going to provide you with a useful list of questions. So this is something you will have to create on your own. The first step is to find out what is already available. It is likely that someone in your organization, at one time or another created a list of questions. When I first started out in my sales career, my sales manager handed me two pages of questions. It was a good starting point, but the questions were not organized in a useful way and did not match my speaking style.

The next step is interviewing your sales manager, top sales professionals, trainers, and anyone else in your organization willing to talk to you. One salesperson I interviewed spent two weeks shadowing one of the top salespeople in his company. His singular focus was to learn questioning methodology. Find out what questions top salespeople in your company ask, in which situations, to which people. Are there different variations of the same questions that are more effective than others? Are there situations where you shouldn't ask certain questions? What are the anticipated answers? This discovery process will aid you in developing a comprehensive list.

Next, develop your own list. Organize it into sections that make it easy to find questions based on your position in the sales cycle, the buyer's job title, product or service type, problem, or situation. Write the questions out the way you would say them—in your own style. Be sure to include possible follow-up questions.

Finally, practice. The only true way to become competent with your questions is to practice on real customers in real time. Yes, it will be awkward at first and you will make mistakes. When I first created my list of questions I carried it with me everywhere I went. At lunch and between appointments I practiced my questions out loud and tried to memorize them. Before each sales call, I reviewed my list and focused on the questions I wanted to ask. Once I was in front of my prospect, I used my list as a resource to be sure I stayed on track.

At first, it was hard. I stumbled on my words, made embarrassing mistakes, and sounded like a robot.

Dual-process questioning wasn't in my vocabulary. I just went down the list. By sticking with it, day in and day out, though, it became second nature. I did not have to think as hard, and I started sounding authentic. Soon, I knew what to ask in just about any situation, including follow-up questions. And after a few months, I didn't need my list anymore. I had memorized and internalized my questions until they were just a part of who I was.

Overcoming Questioning Roadblocks

There are certain people who have their walls up so high that they are nearly impossible to engage. Their answers to your questions are short and clipped and they refuse to reveal anything more than basic facts.

Scott was the vice president of human resources for a large bread and baking company in North Carolina. Tyler was in standing in Scott's office because Scott was the decision maker at the third largest prospect in Tyler's territory. The problem was, Scott's company had been doing business with Tyler's competitor for nearly 20 years. According to Tyler, "That kind of loyalty was beyond rare in my industry and made gaining his business a long-shot at best. There was a great deal at stake. The way contracts worked in my industry, if I lost the sale, I wouldn't have another shot at it for at least five years."

After a quick introduction, Scott and Tyler got down to business. "He'd told me on the phone that he was relatively happy but was willing to give me a few minutes. I explained that my objective for the meeting was just to get to know him better. He said that was fine but that I was just wasting my time because they were happy where they were."

"During our first meeting I tried everything I could to get him talking, but I was getting nothing out of him. He gave me the particulars of the agreement they had in place with my competitor and told me to come back with a proposal. At that point I was beginning to think Scott was right about wasting my time. As I was getting ready to leave I mentioned to him that I'd never seen bread made and asked if he would please give me a tour of the plant. To my surprise, he agreed."

"As soon as we walked out on the production floor his whole demeanor changed. He became animated and talkative. He was excited to show off a new piece of equipment they had just installed. The place was huge and as we walked around he talked, not only about the plant, but about his family and interests outside of work. The most important part of the walk-through was the relationship building. I also found plenty of areas where my competitor was failing."

"At the end of the plant tour I thanked Scott profusely. It really had been fascinating. We had hit it off, and I now had lots of ammunition for my presentation. Then, and I'll never forget this, he invited me to the company golf tournament the next week. A month later I closed the account."

When decision makers are sitting behind their desks, they are in a position of power. Besides the emotional walls they put up, the desks themselves become barriers. However, when you get them out of their offices and walking around, it is much easier to connect. In Tyler's case, as long as Scott was in his office, he was closed to connecting. However, when he was walking around the plant with Tyler by his side, things were more equal, which made conversation easier. Tyler gave Scott something easy to talk about—the plant and bread making process—and that made all the difference. Tyler was genuinely interested in how bread was made and he gave Scott his attention. Scott felt appreciated and important. The more Tyler listened, the more Scott talked. A connection was made, which opened the door to questioning, problem solving, and a sale.

Connecting the Dots

We should not forget that selling is a process. Put simply, a process is a repeatable set of steps that, when followed, leads us to our strategic or tactical objective. In sales, for example, the most simple process is:

Step 1: Qualify
Step 2: Needs analysis/ Information gathering

Step 3: Presentation
Step 4: Close

As the complexity of sales increases, so do the sub-steps. There are dozens of popular sales-process models including Spin Selling, Miller-Heiman, and Sandler. Many large companies have developed their own sales process. No matter where I am speaking, salespeople and their managers ask me which selling methodology I think is best. My answer is always the same, "The one that works for you."

In *People Buy You,* solving problems is where process meets emotion. This is where you gather information about problems, develop solutions based on your product or service, and present those solutions to your prospect. Uncovering problems is the most difficult part of the sales process. Once you have your customer's real problems in hand though, you have to develop and be able to articulate, verbally and in writing, how your product or service will solve each problem. You need to show your customer how your solution will create value or benefit them. The process that works best for this is:

- **Articulate your customer's unique problem:** Mary, in human resources, is spending 30 hours a week on payroll-related issues. This is keeping her from managing benefits enrollment.

- **Recommend a solution:** We recommend implementing the HR Pro 1000 software package, which will fully automate your payroll process.
- **Show them the planned result (value):** Mary will be free to spend her time enrolling employees in the benefits plan, which will save you $22,000 a year in part-time labor and improve morale.

Once you know your customer's problems, it should be fairly easy to develop solutions. Sometimes you may need to get creative, but in most cases the problems are the same ones many of your customers have. Never forget that each person see's his or her problems, no matter how common, as unique. For this reason your presentation of *recommended solutions* and *planned results* must be personalized. You must articulate it in a way that makes your customer feel that the solution is special and specific to them. Always tie your recommendations and value statements back to the emotional hot buttons they revealed during questioning. The impact of this is tremendous, because once again your customer will feel listened to, valued, and important.

Sales Tip: What about Closing?

Salespeople constantly ask me questions about closing. How do I close...? What can I do to close...? Do you have any tricks for closing? Sales managers complain that their salespeople don't know how to close: "The only thing wrong with Johnny is he can't close."

Here's my advice. Don't waste your time learning closing tricks and techniques. The people who want to learn about closing techniques are just looking for shortcuts so they don't have to do the hard work of building relationships and following the sales process. They think that, if they somehow find the right line, all they'll have to do is flash a smile, repeat the magic closing words, and deals will come flying in by the truckload.

I've got news for you. There is no magic closing pill. The fact is, if you have connected, uncovered real problems, presented well thought out solutions that are personalized to your clients, and built some trust along the way, you won't have to worry about closing. All you need to do is ask, "When would you like to get started?" and you'll have all the business you can take.

Summary

Solving problems is the foundation of the *People Buy You* philosophy. Solving problems is about helping other people get what they want. When you help others get what they want, you will get what you want. The key to uncovering and solving problems is questioning and listening deeply. This requires both intellect and empathy. When you connect with your buyer emotionally, by demonstrating empathy, the door will be opened for you to ask deeper questions. Using fluid, dual-process questioning allows you the flexibility to adjust your questions strategically as you uncover the problems that are most emotional and pressing to your buyer. It is then that you gain the insight to build a bridge that links your buyer's problems to your organization's solutions. Never forget, though, that each person sees his or her problems, no matter how common, as unique. For this reason your presentation of *recommended solutions* and *planned results* must be personalized. You must articulate it in a way that makes your customer feel that the solution you have recommended is special and specific to him or to her.

6

Build Trust

Rena sells medical devices for a well-respected national company. She is consistently ranked the number-one salesperson in her organization, outselling more than three hundred of her peers. This is an enviable accomplishment in and of itself, but it gets much more interesting when, as the late Paul Harvey used to say, you hear the rest of her story.

The medical device industry is populated by a group of very intelligent sales professionals. These individuals have the talent to relate to doctors and their staffs. They must understand complicated medical terms, become familiar with complex procedures, and have intimate knowledge of the products they sell. Many of these professionals regularly sit in on surgeries to advise the doctors and nurses who use the instruments they sell. It is an industry where the vast majority of these elite sales professionals work face to face with the medical professionals they serve.

That's what makes Rena unique. She sells medical devices over the phone. She is part of a small team her company initially put together as an experiment. No one expected the kind of performance Rena has delivered. What I found impressive is these are not small transactions. The instruments she sells cost $1,000 to $3,000 each and it is not unusual for a single order to be $20,000 or more.

During our interview, the first question I asked her was, "How in the world are you able to sell such high cost, highly technical products over the phone?"

She told me that, instead of focusing on the product or price, she concentrates on the relationship. "The biggest issue I face selling over the phone is trust. People don't want to take a risk on someone they can't see face-to-face and who they don't know. So I take it slow and work on them a little at a time. It's really about being consistent. I want them to get to know me as a person first. Once they do, things like price don't matter so much."

As I got to know her, I learned that most of her accounts started out really small. Her first step was to persistently work to get at least one doctor at a hospital to buy from her. Then she was relentless in her follow-up. "I want them to know that I'm going to take very good care of them. Anything they need—I'm on top of it."

Her largest customer, and the source of a large percentage of her income, is a hospital where she started out with a single doctor. "He was all I had for two years. This doctor was really loyal to me because whenever he needed anything or had a rush order, I did whatever it took to make it happen. I made it very easy to work with me. Plus, I knew all about him and his family, so we had something to talk about, other than surgical instruments, when I called to follow up. Then, one day, another doctor needed specialized instruments, and my competitor was unable to deliver. My doctor referred him to me. We spoke and I got in touch with the purchasing department. We delivered on time. Now I had two doctors (she was smiling). Then, one day, the head of purchasing at the hospital called me. We struck a deal and my company became the primary vendor for the hospital. I had ten times the business over night, and I made a bunch of new friends."

That's when she leaned across the table and said, "When customers trust you, the selling part is easy."

A Foundation of Trust

When your customers rely on you to deliver on promises, they are putting themselves in a vulnerable position with their money and time. In many cases, their reliance on you creates such vulnerability that, should you fail to perform, the impact on their business, company, or career could be extreme.

Adding to this vulnerability is the fact that, in most business relationships, the ability of one party to completely control the actions of the other party is limited.

Though the tolerance for risk is different for everyone, we generally abhor the unknown. Because of this, it is in our nature as humans to want to control the world around us. Although there are those who are considered control freaks, everyone to one extent or another takes every opportunity to exert control over the variables in their life and business. Frustratingly, the actions of other people are among the many things that, regardless of our efforts, cannot be controlled. We have all experienced the emotional, and, in some cases, financial pain as a result of being burned by or having our trust broken by another person. Beginning in childhood, when we first experience the pain of broken trust and into adulthood, as these experiences become cumulative, we carry skepticism and suspicion into our relationships as a means of protecting ourselves from vulnerability.

The paradox is, for the most part, we really want to trust others. Suspicion and skepticism are uncomfortable feelings. Trust feels good. Trust is stability—a state of well-being we long for. Some people give the gift of trust much more freely than others, who, for lack of better words, are perpetually living in the "show-me state." Most people, however, given enough consistent evidence that you keep your word and do what you say you'll do, will begin to trust you. Ed is a top sales professional in the minerals industry. In Ed's niche, long-term relationships are the key to survival. He said to me, "When people trust you a little, they'll usually find a way to buy something, just to see if you'll do what you say you will. When you deliver on your promises, their trust in you grows, and as trust grows so will your sales."

Building and maintaining trust in business relationships means providing *consistent* evidence that you can be trusted. Steven R. Covey, author of *Seven Habits of Highly Effective People,* likens building trust to making deposits in an "emotional bank account." Using this metaphor, Covey explains that you build trust by making regular deposits (consistent evidence that you are trustworthy) in another person's emotional bank account. As you make deposits, like keeping commitments and delivering on promises, the balance of trust in the account grows. When you fail to honor commitments, renege on promises, make the other person feel unimportant or unappreciated, behave in an unlikable or inconsistent way, you make withdrawals. The theory is, by making regular deposits, trust will be maintained, and there will be greater tolerance for your future indiscretions or mistakes. However, like any bank account, when you make too many withdrawals and allow your account balance to become overdrawn, there are penalties. You lose trust and place the relationship in jeopardy.

Though many factors contribute to the trust your prospects, customers, managers, and peers have in you, the important take-away from this metaphor is, in business and sales, trust is something you earn. In Covey's metaphor, each relationship begins with a neutral balance. I believe that twenty-first-century business relationships begin in the *red*. We enter business relationships because we are motivated by the value or return on investment we receive for the effort we put into the relationship. Until trust is established, each party in the relationship is suspicious of the motivations of the other party. Because of this you are almost always starting off in a hole (especially in sales). This is why you must lay a foundation of trust with consistent evidence that you are trustworthy.

Trust is the foundation on which the business relationships you build rest. Every action, decision, and behavior links to and directly affects trust—positively or negatively. Without trust there is no relationship. You will not close deals or be given new opportunities. Without trust your employees and the people on your support staff will not give you their best work. You will not earn promotions or raises. Without trust there is no loyalty. There will be no repeat business. You will not get referrals. Without trust, your reputation suffers. Here is the bottom line: No matter how likable you are or how connected you are, how many problems you solve, or how many nice things you do, you absolutely, positively cannot do business without trust.

Status Quo Is King

In our risk-averse business world, status quo is king. Whether you are trying to persuade others to accept new ideas, influence a prospect to change vendors, coax a customer to purchase a new product, appeal to a company to adopt a new system, or train a team of people to accept a new process, the greater emotional pull, no matter how illogical, will always be back toward the status quo. We even use sayings like, "Don't fix what isn't broken," to support our desire to remain within the status quo. For salespeople, despite all the concern about their competition, the status quo is and will always be their most formidable competitor. Even in untenable situations in which change is necessary for survival, people will cling to the status quo with sayings like, "Better the devil you know than the devil you don't."

Remember that people prefer stability (status quo) over instability (the unknown). Fear, uncertainty, and doubt of the unknown or the consequences of making a poor decision are a powerful emotional magnet that keeps decision makers holding tight to the status quo. Although few decisions are completely risk free, trust plays a key role in reducing fear and minimizing risk for decision makers. The more they trust you, the higher the probability that they will buy from you or accept your ideas for change. Trust, above all things, trumps status quo.

You Are Always on Stage

A trap many salespeople fall into early on in a business relationship is assuming they have more trust in the emotional bank account than they really do. They falsely believe that charm, charisma, and likability are more important than showing up to meetings on time, being prepared, meeting deadlines, and keeping sales material pristine.

As I stated earlier, most people want to find reasons to trust you. Though you may develop an emotional connection with your prospect by being likable, polite, and charming, you must still earn their trust. Even as they feel more connected to you, every behavior and every action is being scrutinized and analyzed to justify their emotions with facts.

Imagine standing on a stage in an auditorium. In the audience are your clients and their support staffs, your new boss, all your prospects, and your peers. Every behavior is being watched. You are being observed to see if your actions are congruent with your words. Perhaps you are polite to some people, but not others. Perhaps you become agitated at a minor inconvenience. Maybe you were late to a meeting and did not call in advance or didn't return an e-mail or voice mail in a timely manner. You could have missed a key piece of information that your client asked you to remember. Maybe your presentations materials or samples were not in pristine condition Your business card had stains on it. You told a little white lie and got caught. Your actions are being compared to the others on the stage. Judgments are being made about how much to trust you.

In sales and business, you are always on stage, and it is essential that you control the behaviors you allow others to observe. You must exert a tremendous amount of self-discipline to manage every behavior, promise, and action while in front of your audience. This is where the rubber meets the road. This is where emotion collides with logic.

Buyers are going to do everything possible to minimize risk. In most cases, the status quo is a lower risk than buying something from you. Therefore, your imperative is to reduce the fear your buyer feels by demonstrating with your actions (what they see you do) that buying from you will solve their problem and be a low-risk decision. Again the foundation of trust is built one brick at a time based on the consistent and ongoing evidence others have that you are trustworthy.

Going the Extra Mile

Not long ago I had the privilege of hearing a speech by Coach Pat Dye, the former head coach of the Auburn University football team. This is a man who pulled himself up from the dirt roads of the rural south to coach championship football teams in the Southeastern Conference. Toward the end of his talk he said, "Listen closely because I'm going to tell you how to become special."

I looked around and all of the people in the audience leaned forward. No one wanted to miss this secret. Coach Dye paused for a moment and looked over the audience. Then he spoke, "There are two parts of anything you do in life: *the first mile and the extra mile*. Most people do a good job in the first mile. They work hard and do the right things. But it is what you do in the extra mile that makes you special. In the extra mile you go beyond just being good. You give more, work harder, hustle, practice longer, overcome obstacles, and do the things that others are unwilling to do."

Later, at lunch, I had an opportunity to spend some time with Gary, a successful sales professional who sells products to the manufacturing industry. He has been a top producer for nearly 20 years. It did not take long to figure out that he goes the extra mile in everything he does. During our conversation, he told me about a recent vacation during which he spent an afternoon working to ensure that the installation crew from his company was taking care of one of his new customers—a customer, by the way, that he had pursued for five years. "It made my new customer very happy. So happy that they placed another order." Most people would have turned their phone off and dealt with the issue when they returned from vacation. People who go the extra mile always give more. Gary's new customer watched his actions.. When they observed that he was committed to following through on his promises, they bought more. He provided evidence that he could be trusted.

Going the extra mile is a commitment to excellence. It is the willingness and discipline to do the right thing even when no one is watching. People who go the extra mile put their customers before commissions. They always give more than required. Going the extra mile sets you apart from 90 percent of your competitors. It lifts you up in the eyes of others and it builds trust. Going the extra mile (demonstrating your commitment to excellence) has a huge impact on decision making, both consciously and subconsciously with buyers. When buyers embrace the status quo or are afraid of making a poor decision, going the extra mile counteracts their fears and creates feelings of well-being about you and the decision to buy your products or services.

One of my favorite sayings is, "There are no traffic jams on the extra mile." Going the extra mile is an attitude, driven by your internal belief system. It is a commitment to excellence in everything you do—even when no one is looking. It is realizing that most contests are won by small margins, and that the winner is almost always the competitor who maintained the self-discipline to give more in the face of adversity and exhaustion. Going the extra mile is something that happens on the inside first and then manifests itself in your external actions. By providing consistent evidence that you always give and do more than required, over time, you build a rock-solid foundation of trust.

Sweat the Small Stuff

When it comes to trust, little things make a big difference. Although there are situations in which one big lapse in judgment injures trust to such an extent that there is no going back, these events are rare. As a rule it is the culmination of many small breaches that weaken or destroy the foundation of trust.

Things such as showing up late for meetings, not returning phone calls, disorganization, missing deadlines, spelling and grammatical errors on written documents, being unprepared for meetings, inaccurate facts, inconsiderate behavior, and failure to follow up, all seem very small. However, over time they add up and build the case that you cannot be trusted.

In business relationships, and, in particular, in new relationships, you simply cannot afford the luxury of a slip up. Go back to that picture of yourself on stage with everyone watching. Use this as motivation to put systems in place to keep you organized, manage your time, and ensure that you do everything with perfection.

Sales Tip: Perfection Is the Winning Edge

Spectators at the 2006 Indianapolis 500 witnessed one of the most spectacular finishes in the history of the race. Sam Hornish edged out Marco Andretti to win by .0635 second. For his victory, Hornish took home $1,744,855. By comparison, Marco Andretti's second place winnings were $698,505. Hornish earned more than twice what Andretti took home by beating him by six-hundredths of a second. That is a hugely disproportionate payout for such a minuscule margin of victory. It almost doesn't seem fair! But it happens every day in sporting events and business. Most contests are won and lost by very thin margins, but the difference in the reward for winning or the penalty for losing is large.

So how did Hornish manage to gain the winning edge? What made the difference between him and Andretti? There is simply no way to know exactly what gave Hornish the .0635 edge to victory. It could have been anything or a combination of many things. We could work back through his team's activities preparing for and executing the race, but we would never discover a definitive answer.

In the end, the difference between Hornish and Andretti is that Sam Hornish just did more things right. In other words, he was perfect more often than Andretti, and the result was a slim margin of victory and a huge margin of payout.

(continued)

(Continued)

What's the point? In business, there are always tough competitors, there is a great deal at stake, and the margin of victory is almost always slim. Everything you do has the potential to change the outcome in the win or loss column. In sales, unlike car racing, a loss most often means walking away empty-handed. The winner, most often, is the person who does more things perfectly, refuses to take shortcuts, and has the self-discipline to go the extra mile.

Simply stated, to win, you must be perfect in everything. Your interpersonal interactions, questions, collateral, and presentation must be perfect. Every detail, from the way you dress, smile, walk, talk, the cleanliness of your car, organization of your materials, and your manners must be perfect. You should do nothing to call your trustworthiness into question. Although you may never know what the winning edge is, you can always be sure that the winner does more things perfectly than the loser.

Leverage Your Support Team

There are few lone wolves in business these days. To one extent or another, you count on other people for support. The most successful sales professionals have learned how to leverage their support teams to build trust with prospects and customers. They maintain ongoing strategic relationships with the people in their companies who have the resources and know-how to back them up in the sales process with competitive research, presales engineering, custom sales collateral and presentations, product research and comparison, supply chain and forecasting, team presentations, financing, implementation, and much more. By involving a diverse group of people who have specialization in key areas, they are able to offer more robust and relevant solutions to their customers' problems. Because they delegate key tasks to their support staff, they have more time to spend developing the relationship.

Utilizing your support staff effectively requires that the moment a new opportunity enters your pipeline, you begin mapping the sales process and answering core questions about decision makers, influencers, competitors, products and services, and your engagement methodology. When it comes to strategy, I am a fan of Miller-Heiman's Strategic Selling methodology. No matter what works best for you, planning and organizing by asking and answering key questions up front is critical. It ensures that, when you do go to your support staff for help, you know what to ask for and you respect their time by having ready the information they need.

Once you have your team engaged, you must provide consistent and ongoing communication. One of my favorite sayings is "In God we trust, everyone else we follow up on." Communication is critical because it ensures that your sales support team remains engaged in your deal and keeps the ball moving forward. It demonstrates that you care and keeps you connected to the people you need on your side. Regular communication also gives you the opportunity to provide positive feedback and appreciation. This, in turn, motivates the support staff to work even harder for you. Far too many salespeople fail to communicate on a regular basis and find themselves scrambling at the last moment because critical tasks were left undone or incomplete. These same salespeople are quick to point the finger at their support staff when, in reality, they have no one to blame but themselves. Because you get the commissions, you bear the responsibility to consistently communicate and follow up—not the other way around.

I've always been appalled at business professionals who treat the support staff with indifference. Even worse are those who are demanding and rude—especially with last-minute requests that create disruption and inconvenience to people they need on their side. Use the *People Buy You* levers to build relationships with your support team. Remember that the people on your support team are people just like you. They want to be respected, to do worthwhile work, and to feel important and appreciated. Take the time to get to know the people on the support team individually. Find out what makes them tick. Understand how they are compensated, how they like to operate, and where they have the most experience. Give them the same respect you yourself would like to receive. And, above all, be sure to thank them for the work they do.

Failures by your support staff to deliver on commitments are a blow to the foundation of trust you have with your clients. Therefore, you must take responsibility and accountability for their actions. This requires both the strategic planning I mentioned earlier, and leadership. You must understand, though, that leading a support team is not like managing employees. In most cases these people don't work for you and you do not have the authority to tell them what to do. Instead you must convince your sales support team to work in your best interest, not because they have to, but because they want to.

It is your commitment to plan and organize around strategic objectives; it is your self-discipline to communicate and follow up effectively; it is your work to build and maintain relationships that make them want to help you. And, with the respect and trust you have developed through the relationships you built along the way, you'll find that leveraging your corporate resources is a powerful way to build trust and overcome the status quo.

Response

Few people expect you or your company to be perfect. They realize sooner or later things will go wrong.

But if they do not expect perfection they do expect a rapid and timely response. When there is a question, problem, concern, service interruption, or issue of any kind and your prospect, customer, boss, or peer reaches out to you by phone or in writing, you have a golden opportunity to build trust.

It seems counterintuitive that by making a mistake you can actually cement your business relationships. Remember though that people are watching you, looking for evidence that you can be trusted. When people call you for help, they have an opportunity to observe you in action. When your response is swift, you solve their problem, and your follow-up communication is timely, you then provide clear evidence that you are trustworthy.

Admit When You Are Wrong and Apologize

Sooner or later you are going to screw up and let someone down. Things like failing to keep a commitment, having to go back on a promise, or missing a meeting or scheduled call shouldn't happen, but they sometimes do. When you make a mistake, face up to the situation as quickly as possible and apologize. Apologies and admitting where you have been wrong provide others with the opportunity to observe your character. Sincere apologies are accepted and appreciated, and they demonstrate your integrity (provided you are not apologizing for the same mistake again and again).

Some years ago Denise, a uniform-services sales rep, was sitting across from Ron, the senior purchasing manager at a Fuji Film plant in South Carolina. Her face was flushed with embarrassment. It had taken months to get the appointment and now—total disaster. With her sales manager sitting right next to her, she had watched in horror as Ron pulled a disposable *Kodak* camera out of the package in front of him. The package he was holding was part of a marketing promotion sent out by Denise's corporate office to highly valued prospects. The idea was that the prospect would take a picture of the uniforms their employees were wearing and send it back to get a prize (which would be delivered, of course, by the salesperson). It had been a successful promotion, but this faux pas was beyond embarrassing.

Ron placed the camera on the table and said, "You all should be more careful what you send. Would you please take this with you when you go?" Denise and her sales manager apologized profusely, but the conversation that followed was terse. Denise could not believe her bad luck. It had taken blood, sweat, and tears to get this appointment. Now, because of a dumb mistake, she had no chance with the account.

On the way back to the office, her sales manager had an idea. "He explained that we needed a more creative apology to get back on Ron's good side. He said we needed to make him laugh because it was kind of funny. I wasn't laughing but I was up for anything that would get us back in the door."

"We stopped and bought a bunch of Fuji disposable cameras and then called the marketing department and had them send us an empty promotional package."

"My sales manager's idea was simple. We sat down in his office and together wrote a self-deprecating poem about our unfortunate screwup. It was hilarious. Then we took a picture of ourselves surrounded by the Fuji Film cameras. We had it developed and put the poem, the picture of us, and a Fuji Film camera in the promotional package and overnighted it to Ron. I was on pins and needles the next day when I called him to be sure he received the package. He was laughing when he answered the phone, and with a pleasant voice said, 'Apology accepted. When do you want to come back?' After that, we developed a very open relationship. Ron would always take my phone calls, and he treated me with respect and kindness. That apology changed everything, and I eventually landed the account."

Often, apologies, just as in Denise's story, make relationships stronger when approached the right way. The keys are humility (put your pride aside), timeliness, and sincerity. A little humor or creativity, especially in an embarrassing situation, can go a long way.

Listening Builds Trust

Unlike likability, which can happen instantly, trust is something that is built over time. However, if there is a fast track to trust, it is listening. The more you listen to another person, the more they will trust you. Years ago I had a sales rep working for me who consistently sold more than anyone in my entire region. I went to see him to find out what he was doing. Billy explained that he had gone through the files and located ex-customers who were now doing business with our competitors. Most of our salespeople wouldn't get near previous customers with a ten-foot pole! Most often ex-customers had left us due to a complaint about price, product, or service deficiency. Calling them would just get you an earful of all the reasons they hated us.

Billy relished the calls, "I take the issue head-on." He said, "I ask them straight up to tell me why they quit. They've all got a story, and I just listen to them. When they figure out that I'm not going to interrupt or argue, they talk even more. Eventually, after they've run out of negative things to say about their experience with us, they'll start complaining about the company that has their business now. I just keep listening. Pretty soon what made them unhappy with us doesn't sound so bad when compared with the problems they have with our competitor. When the time is right,

I explain what we have changed and how. Then, with the information they just gave me, I structure a new program that solves their problems. Most of them come back. I think all they really wanted was someone to listen to them."

Billy listened and did not judge, argue, or interrupt. This provided evidence that he was trustworthy. The more he listened, the more he was trusted. Soon the ex-customer, who had every reason not to trust him, felt comfortable enough to reveal that they were very unhappy with our competitor, which opened the door to winning them back.

Consistent Behavior

Inconsistent behavior is a red flag when it comes to trust. When you are unpredictable, it is hard for people to trust you. This brings us full circle to the metaphor of business as a stage. Upon this stage, your behaviors are front and center. When you act out of character (for example, if you normally have a relaxed, professional demeanor but in a moment of irritation lose your temper), it affects your clients' trust in you. If repeated, these instances combine to crumble your foundation of trust. Inconsistent behavior can cause irreparable damage. As we are all aware, it has derailed promising careers, ruined political campaigns, and sunk many business deals. You control what others are allowed to observe. Think before you speak. Learn to pause and consider the consequence of rash action. With trust, you do not get the luxury of relaxing and letting your guard down. You are always on stage.

Summary

Without trust you cannot effectively conduct business. It is the foundation on which all relationships rest. To build and maintain trust in business relationships, you must provide *consistent* evidence that you can be trusted. In sales and business, you are always on stage. Therefore, it is essential that you control the behaviors you allow others to observe. You must exert a tremendous amount of self-discipline to manage every behavior, promise, and action while in front of others. It is essential that you develop the discipline to consistently manage your behaviors, follow through on commitments, and keep your promises.

7

Create Positive Emotional Experiences

I'd been on the road for three solid weeks speaking at national sales meetings, training businesspeople, and working on consulting gigs. January had been completely overbooked. As I sat in the Burbank airport on a Friday evening, looking up at the word DELAYED displayed next to my flight, I was kicking myself for scheduling a two-day, weekend training event in San Jose. I'd squeezed this one in between a national sales meeting keynote in Los Angeles and another national sales meeting in Orlando the following Monday. I'd been jumping from city to city for almost a month with no break and no time to go home. I was exhausted, and my attitude had taken a downturn. It did not get any better once I finally made it onto my flight. I would have done anything to get out of this

147

commitment. I could not believe how stupid I was for agreeing to do this. The money was not worth it.

By the time I got off of the plane in San Jose at 8 P.M. I was exasperated. Pulling my travel-worn roller bag behind me, I made my way out of the terminal to grab a cab and get to my hotel. But then I saw a sign with my name on it. Seriously—a sign with my name on it! I did a double take just to be sure. There, standing before me, was the CEO of the company holding the sign waiting for me. I tried not to look shocked; I managed a smile and reached out to shake her hand. "I wasn't expecting a reception."

Cheri smiled back, "I know how tough it is to spend a weekend away from home and thought you might like a ride. Can I buy you dinner?"

We walked out to the parking garage and loaded my bags into the back of her SUV. Then I walked around to the passenger side and opened the door. If you are anything like me, the passenger seat of your car probably has some junk on it. In my car it serves as a desk. When people ride with me, I have to go through the ritual of emptying the passenger seat so they have a place to sit. So when I opened the door of Cheri's car and saw things on the passenger seat, I politely waited for her to move them. On the seat was what appeared to be a birthday gift, a couple of bottles of water, and some energy bars. But as I stood there waiting, she made no effort to move the items from the seat.

Finally she looked at me and said, "That's for you. I thought you might need a refreshment after your trip."

I was immediately touched by her thoughtfulness. I started to feel guilty for my poor attitude. I thanked her for her kindness, gathered the items up, and sat down. Then I held out the birthday present and asked her if I should put it in the back seat. She shook her head and said, "No, that's for you."

"But it's not my birthday." I protested.

"Well, you have a birthday, don't you?"

"Yes, I guess I do."

"Then, happy birthday."

By now I was grinning from ear to ear. Getting a surprise gift felt great. Suddenly I was energized. My positive attitude was restored. "May I open it?"

She was grinning now, too. "Of course."

Inside the package was a popular new book I'd been meaning to pick up. I'd mentioned it during our last conversation, and she had remembered. I was touched by her gesture and blown away that a virtual stranger could be so kind.

That exchange created an instant connection. It also motivated me to work as hard as I had ever worked for a client. I gave them everything I had and more. Over the next year, I remained focused on Cheri's company, helping them develop new growth strategies. I made regular follow-up calls and did impromptu coaching. Much of the work I did after our initial meeting was not billed. I gave them my time because it made me feel good to repay the kindness Cheri had shown me.

The Law of Reciprocity

Now I'm not advocating that anyone work for free. I shared this story to illustrate the true power of *creating positive emotional experiences* for others. In his classic book, *Ultimate Success*, Frank Beaudine writes that the Law of Reciprocity is one of the great truths of life, because the more we give, the more we receive. Robert B. Cialdini, author of *The Psychology of Persuasion*, goes a step further, saying, "One of the most potent of the weapons of influence around us is the [law] for reciprocation. The [law] says that we should try to repay, in kind, what another person has provided us." In layman's terms, the Law of Reciprocity simply explains that when someone gives you something, you feel an obligation to give value back.

Notice that, even though the Law of Reciprocity says that when you give to others they will *feel an obligation* to give back, it does not say they *will* give back. Some people may never return your goodwill. This is why the deliberate pursuit of reciprocity, in other words, approaching reciprocity as a transaction—I give value to you, therefore, you give equal or greater value back—does not work. Doing so will leave you jaded and frustrated because having these expectations are, in many ways, just premeditated resentments. What does work is creating positive emotional experiences for others because you sincerely want to give them joy with no expectation for anything in return. This requires faith that, when you give with sincerity and for the right reasons, the universe has an amazing way of evening things out and paying you back many times over—sometimes directly and sometimes indirectly.

Unfortunately, far too many people choose to ignore this universal truth and instead live by the motto, "Me first." I'm sure you know who these *takers* are in your life. They argue that they've "tried to give help to others, but it doesn't work because everyone is just out to take advantage of them." They have no faith in the Law of Reciprocity. In sales and business, the me-first attitude has significant and negative impact on relationships and long-term earning potential. Many salespeople view their prospects, customers, employers, and peers as mere paychecks. They consider business relationships as a means to an end. Instead of becoming genuinely interested in solving their customers' problems, delivering value, or helping others, they are genuinely interested in getting the sale, getting the paycheck, or getting something else they want. Of course we all have examples of people who have been rewarded, at least temporarily, for their take-first attitude. In spite of this, the one thing I can tell you with certainty is that what goes around, comes around.

For everyone and everything, eventually, the scales will balance.

Anchoring

In sales and business, the Law of Reciprocity is your ally because you can use it to anchor your relationships. At sea, an anchor creates a bond between the ocean floor and a vessel. A big metal hook on the ocean floor is attached to the ship by a chain. That bond holds the vessel stationary and safe.

It is important to note that anchors cannot be dropped to the ocean floor and forgotten. Captains must relentlessly monitor their anchors to ensure they are holding fast and not dragging. Constant changes in wind, currents, tide, and the sea floor all conspire to unhook the anchor and leave the ship adrift—a disaster waiting to happen.

Relationships must be anchored, too. In relationships, an anchor creates an emotional bond between you and another person. This aids in holding the relationship together and safe. Likewise, the emotional anchors that hold your relationships firm require the same vigilance. Relationships that are ignored eventually go adrift.

Sadly, many salespeople think that after they get the sale the customer will keep buying because he or she likes the product or service. They've fooled themselves into believing that their product, service, process, or price is unique and the customer will keep buying for that reason. However, most customers don't see things that way. To them, all are equal. Few salespeople have not heard the words (in one form or another), "All you guys are the same." The brutal fact is, as soon as you forget to appreciate your client, someone else will. In the *People Buy You* world, if you lose that connection, you are toast. The reality is that, when you close a deal, there are 10 more salespeople standing behind you selling the same or similar products or services. Never forget your customer bought *you*. Products can be duplicated but *you* cannot. However, if you don't keep your customers thinking about *you*, sooner or later some other person will come along and win them over.

There is a saying, *always leave them wanting more.* This saying is applied most often to performers who work on the stage—actors, speakers, musicians, and comedians. This line is just as appropriate to business professionals. By now I'm beginning to sound like a broken record (for those of you who remember what a record is). Nevertheless, it is essential that you never forget that as a business professional you are always on stage. If you want to close more deals, maintain long-term relationships, retain your clients, and keep your career upwardly mobile, you must strive in every interaction to leave others wanting more. Many buyers would rather spend an hour in the dentist's chair getting a root canal than an hour with a salesperson.

But, what if your customers really looked forward to your calls or visits? What if your customers told your competitors that they would never leave you? What if they were more forgiving of inevitable shortfalls and service issues? Calls and meetings would be very different if people were eager to meet with you. Just think how this would neutralize the efforts of your competitors to steal your clients. All of this is possible *and more* when you create Positive Emotional Experiences.

Creating positive emotional experiences anchors you to others. When you do nice things for prospects, customers, employees, and peers, you improve your connections and build trust, and others will naturally feel obligated to give something back to you. In business relationships, what is given back may be in the direct form of additional business, referrals, or signed contracts. I remind you, though, that you must never create positive emotional experiences for others with the expectation of a direct payback.

The more powerful obligation that others give in return for the nice things you do for them is loyalty. Where a direct payback may be a one-time event, loyalty is ongoing. You gain loyalty over the long term as positive emotional experiences add up and your client begins to trust that you really care about them. Loyalty locks your competitors out. Loyalty forgives mistakes. Loyalty generates referrals. Loyalty gives you inside information, moves your invoices to the top of the accounts-payable file, gets you past gatekeepers, lends you a hand, whispers in someone's ear. Loyalty goes to battle for you.

It Don't Cost Nuthin' to Be Nice (Little Things Are Big Things)

Consider this story that legendary coach Bear Bryant is said to have told at a touchdown club meeting. In his first year as a coach, and he had gone down into southern Alabama on a recruiting trip. He stopped in at a little roadside dive for lunch. It wasn't much of a place, but Coach Bryant said the food was real good. The owner figured out that the new head coach of the Crimson Tide was in his restaurant. He asked if Coach Bryant would send him an autographed picture to hang on his wall. Coach Bryant wrote the owner's name and address on a napkin, thanked him for lunch, and left.

According to Coach Bryant, "When I got back to Tuscaloosa late that night, I took that napkin from my shirt pocket and put it under my keys so I wouldn't forget it. Back then, I was excited that anybody would want a picture of me. The next day, we found a picture and I wrote on it, 'Thanks for the best lunch I've ever had.'"

Years later, after Coach Bryant had become famous, he was in the same area recruiting a young man he badly wanted for his team. Unfortunately, the kid was dead set on signing with Alabama's archrival, Auburn. Nothing could convince him otherwise, and having done his best, Coach Bryant packed up and went home empty handed.

"Two days later, I'm in my office in Tuscaloosa and the phone rings, and it's this kid who just turned me down, and he says, 'Coach, do you still want me at Alabama?' And I said, 'Yes, I sure do.' And he says, 'Okay, I'll come.' And I say, 'Well, son, what changed your mind?'"

"He said, 'When my grandpa found out that I had a chance to play for you and said no, he pitched a fit and told me I wasn't going nowhere but Alabama, and wasn't playing for nobody but you. He thinks a lot of you and has ever since y'all met.'"

"Well, I didn't know his granddad from Adam's house cat, so I asked him who his granddaddy was and he said, 'You probably don't remember him, but you ate at his restaurant your first year at Alabama and you sent him a picture that he's had hung in that place ever since. That picture's his pride and joy and he still tells everybody about the day that Bear Bryant came in.'

"'My grandpa said that when you left there, he never expected you to remember him or to send him that picture, but you kept your word to him and, to Grandpa, that's everything. He said you could teach me more than football, and I had to play for a man like you, so I guess I'm going to.'"

Coach Bryant went on to say, "I was floored. But I learned that the lessons my mama taught me were always right. 'It don't cost nuthin' to be nice.'"

This story illustrates the lasting impact of small acts of kindness and the sheer power of the Law of Reciprocity. Certainly big experiences, like taking a client who loves NASCAR® into the pit to meet his favorite driver, can cost thousands of dollars and create lasting memories. However, being thoughtful doesn't have to cost much of anything. In many cases small gestures carry far more meaning than big ones. Remembering a client's birthday or important family event, sending a handwritten thank-you note, or leaving a congratulatory voice mail are all easy and essentially free ways to create positive emotional experiences. It is all about being creative, making it personal, and having the self-discipline to follow through.

Develop a Disciplined System

Creating positive emotional experiences means taking action to do something kind for another person for the sole purpose of making them feel good. The discipline to take action, to follow through, is essential. Many people have the intention to create positive emotional experiences. Few have the discipline to follow through. Good intentions mean nothing. Each day you will be presented with opportunities to create positive emotional experiences for others. It will be difficult to leverage these opportunities without a system for follow-up. Your system should be designed to help you stay on track and remember birthdays, anniversaries, and special events. It should have processes that make it easy for you to do things like send handwritten notes. It should also remind you to follow through on random events like finding and sending a book you think your client will like. You should also have a system for planning larger events to ensure the important details that help personalize the event are not forgotten.

Customer Relationship Management Systems

Modern CRM programs like SalesNexus.com, Landslide.com, SalesForce.com, and ACT are all capable of managing this for you. Take copious notes. Record everything in your CRM program. Become systematic and self-disciplined in collecting and recording data that supports your efforts to create unique, personalized, positive emotional experiences.

Assistants

If you are fortunate enough to have an assistant, have them set up a system and delegate as much as possible.

An assistant can perform miracles when it comes to creating positive emotional experiences, while allowing you to remain focused on high-value activities. If you do not have a company-provided assistant, consider hiring a virtual assistant. Virtual assistants work by the hour, are relatively inexpensive, and will take care of many of the little things that make a big difference over time.

Robert Louis Stevenson said, "Don't judge each day by the harvest you reap but by the seeds you plant." The Law of Reciprocity says you have to pay in advance. You only get back after you give. If you don't take action, you get nothing. I wish it were different. I wish that we could blink our eyes, wave a wand, or wiggle our noses and all the hard work of creating positive emotional experiences would be done. As we all know, it doesn't work that way.

Positive Emotional Experiences

Why do I use the term positive emotional experience? Because, what we experience is what we remember. The more emotional the experience, the deeper it is branded in our thoughts. While doing interviews for this book, I heard many unique stories and testimonials about creating positive emotional experiences.

One sales professional I interviewed told me this story. "The decision maker at one the biggest accounts in my territory was the vice president of operations. He had relocated a few years earlier to take the promotion. Over the course of several meetings, I had learned that he really missed home. One thing he missed the most was ribs from the place called the Rendezvous. About a month earlier I'd given him a proposal, but I was getting nowhere with a decision. My numbers were good, and if he bought from me, it would be a big cost savings for his business. For some reason this guy would not get off the ball. He kept telling me that they were having a hard time deciding what to do, and my competitor had asked for a little more time to try to get things right. I was exasperated. This competitor had been screwing them for years. I couldn't understand why he couldn't see it. Suddenly, a light went off! I got the idea to have ribs shipped in from the Rendezvous. I called and asked him to lunch. He agreed and asked where I wanted to go. I said, 'Don't worry about it, I'm bringing it with me.' I had four full slabs and the fix'ns shipped overnight. The next day we had a feast. He said it had been three years since he'd been to the Rendezvous. By the look on his face I could tell he was in hog heaven (pardon the pun). After lunch, he thanked me over and over. I shook his hand and left. I did not ask for the business and in fact we did not talk business at all. It was just two guys having lunch. A week later he called me to say 'congratulations'. He had awarded us the contract."

The creative opportunities to add joy to lives of your prospects, clients, managers, and peers abound. There are hundreds of stories, big and small, that reinforce the power of creating positive emotional experiences for the people around you:

- A phone call to congratulate an accomplishment.
- A handwritten Thank You note.
- Birthday cards.
- Anniversary cards.
- A framed newspaper or magazine clipping of a client receiving an award or article about her company.
- An unexpected gift commemorating a special occasion.
- Concert tickets along with special VIP access.
- Tickets to a major event like the Masters®, World Series, or Daytona 500.
- Unique meals.
- Getting a client access to drive a race car.
- Helping a client's child get an interview, a golf lesson, a meeting with an important person.
- Sending flowers to a funeral.
- Giving an autographed picture of a celebrity.
- A round of golf at an exclusive club.

Positive emotional experiences are deeper and work best in creating emotional anchors when your actions are thoughtful and personal. Knowing the right thing to do in your unique situation only requires that you listen and be creative. One account manager told me about a card she sent to one of her clients. "His wife had just had a baby. I was talking to him one day and he seemed stressed and tired. So I got a funny card and wrote, 'Take some time for yourself. New dads need rest too.' It really touched him. It has been two years and he still thanks me for thinking about him." The opportunities are endless.

Pay Attention to Self-Disclosures (Listen Deeply)

The secret to uncovering opportunities to create personalized, thoughtful positive emotional experiences that make others feel appreciated and valued is listening deeply for self-disclosure. You'll recall that when you listen, others feel more connected to you. The more connected they feel, the more they will reveal about themselves. Focusing all your attention on the person in front of you and listening with your eyes, ears, and heart (empathy) will lead you to the areas that are of emotional importance to them. Focus your attention here, and you quickly find opportunities to create positive emotional experiences for others that have deep emotional significance. The key is to always be on the lookout for opportunities to create positive emotional experiences—both big and small.

Adam is a regional account executive for a Fortune 500 business-services company. A talented and successful sales professional, he has a knack for creating positive emotional experiences for his clients. In one instance, Adam was working on a large complex account with a heavy equipment dealer. Closing the deal meant president's club, a trip to Hawaii, and a big bonus. There was a lot at stake. Each time he met with Cheryl, the purchasing manager, she would talk about her daughter who was playing basketball at the University of Kentucky. She had pictures of her daughter all over her office. Adam could tell that this was a source of deep pride for her. Adam's own daughter, who was much younger, was also a basketball player, so it was an easy conversation.

Adam wanted to do something nice for Cheryl to help build his relationship with her. He considered tickets to a WNBA game for Cheryl and her daughter, but due to company policy, she was unable to accept any gifts—not even lunch. Adam was stumped. The incumbent vendor had a long history and greater access. Adam needed Cheryl on his side to have any chance at the deal. The proposal was due soon and time was running out.

Then it came to him, "I was driving home from an appointment with Cheryl and it hit me. Her biggest source of pride and joy was that her daughter was playing NCAA Division I basketball. I needed to do something that tapped into that emotion. As soon as

I got home I went online and ordered a University of Kentucky logoed basketball. As soon as it arrived I put it in an overnight package, along with a Sharpie® and a note and shipped it to her. In the note I simply asked her if she could get her daughter to autograph the basketball for my daughter. The next day Cheryl called. She was beside herself. She was so excited that I had asked for her daughter's autograph and said her daughter would be thrilled to sign the ball. I met with her two weeks later and she was beaming when she handed me the signed ball. I had avoided the no–gift policy and done something that was way better than taking her to lunch. And, as a bonus, my daughter had a new hero to look up to."

Adam eventually closed the deal. He still had to develop a proposal with real solutions for Cheryl's business problems and create value for her. His creative, personalized gesture built a strong connection with Cheryl that helped him get the information he needed to build the proposal. This act of kindness, which cost less than $50, played a key role in earning him a bonus check in excess of $10,000. It worked because it tapped into the insatiable human desire to feel important. When Adam asked Cheryl for her daughter's autograph, he treated Cheryl and her daughter like celebrities. This created a deep, positive emotional experience for Cheryl. I have no doubt that she told the story over and over to her friends and family. Each time she told the story, she felt more important and more connected to Adam.

This amazing story happened because Adam was listening for important emotional clues. He was tuned into his prospect. Because of this, he discovered an opportunity to make a real impact on Cheryl's life, which, in the end, had an equally important impact on his life.

Sales Tip: Handwritten Notes (Little Things Are Big Things)

It's the same routine. You grab the stack of mail and flip, flip, flip, bill, bill, pre-approved credit card, bill, pre-approved credit card, and then, there it is in all its glory: the Holy Grail of snail mail—the handwritten note. It's the real thing. Blue cursive writing, a familiar name in the upper-left-hand corner, and a genuine United States postage stamp!

You smile with anticipation as you slowly open the envelope and pull out the note card. It feels great. You can't really explain why—it just does. Technology and the speed of communication in the twenty-first century have made the personal note a dying art. Most of us have to think really hard to remember the last time we got one. There is good news, though. In our technology-obsessed world, your simple, handwritten note will

(continued)

(*Continued*)

stand out. Your customers will remember you. They will associate you with the good feeling they received when they pulled your note out of their stack of junk mail.

Little things are big things. For the cost of a postage stamp, a note card, and five minutes of your time, you can create a positive emotional experience that will be appreciated and remembered. Develop the habit of carrying note cards and stamps with you at all times. Set a goal of sending three to five handwritten notes each day. Note cards should be sent within 24 hours after a meeting, event, or if you are thanking the recipient for something specific. Make it a habit to send a handwritten thank you note after every meeting with a customer or prospect. Write the note before your next appointment. Drop your notes in the mailbox at the end of the day. Go to your local printer or online stationer and invest in stationery with your name on it. Use good paper, a conservative font, with your name embossed in black ink. Don't forget the matching envelopes. Your unique, personalized notes will send the message that you go the extra mile in everything you do. Develop a correspondence schedule, ensuring that customers, prospects, friends, and your professional network are touched several times each year.

If you are looking at your schedule, your Black-Berry, the 300 new e-mails you haven't answered yet, and the sales report you owe the boss, and you are thinking to yourself, "Yeah right, like I have time to mail note cards!" Think again. In today's competitive marketplace, you simply cannot afford to be like everyone else. Handwritten notes do require extra effort and discipline (which is why so few people send them). However, with just a little extra effort, handwritten notes will help you connect with future prospects, strengthen your business network, and build stronger personal relationships.

Summary

Creating positive emotional experiences for others allows you to take advantage of the Law of Reciprocity, which states that when you give something of value to others, they will feel obligated to give something to you. When you consistently create joy in the lives of your prospects, customers, managers, and peers, without expecting anything in return, you build emotional bonds or anchors. These anchors create loyalty, which results in new sales, referrals, retention, and repeat business. Developing a system for follow-up and follow-through will help you take consistent action. To uncover the opportunities to provide unique positive emotional experiences for the people around you, listen deeply for emotional clues to what is most important to them. Positive emotional experiences are most effective when personalized to the recipient.

8

A Brand
Called You

Marketers frequently gather current and potential customers into rooms with two-way mirrors to test perceptions of products, services, and brands. These focus groups help them understand the emotional and experiential perceptions their current and potential customers have, relative to their brands. The data gathered in these focus groups is used to refine or redefine products, services, messaging, positioning, and advertising.

Now imagine this. We've gathered a group of your customers, prospects, peers, and managers together in a room. Sitting with the group is a moderator who will ask questions designed to uncover their perceptions of you. Behind the two-way mirror are researchers who will be taking notes on every data point: the words the individuals in the group say, and their expressions, tones of voice, and body language. You have been invited to sit and observe.

What will these people say about you? How will they feel about you? What is their experience with you? Do they find you likable? Will they say you are a problem solver? Do they trust you? Will they say that you care about them? Do they see you as a hard worker? Do you offer value or are you focused on taking value? How do you stack up against your competitors? Are you perceived as different or the same? What would they say you should change or refine? What do they perceive as your strengths? Overall, what is their perception of you as a person? For most people, this exercise would be a frightening or, at least, an extremely uncomfortable experience. Few people would enjoy the criticism, no matter how constructive, a focus group of this sort would generate.

A few years ago I hired a top business coaching firm to help me understand how others perceived me. I wanted to make changes that would ultimately improve my personal brand and grow my business. They assigned a PhD who was an expert in human behavior as my coach. She had years of experience coaching CEOs and senior-level executives in many Fortune 500 companies. The first thing she asked for was a list of clients, business associates, and friends. She then personally interviewed each person on my list and returned with a report that provided a comprehensive picture of how I was perceived by these individuals.

When we sat down together to review the data she gathered, I was crushed. Though my focus group said many very nice things about me, they also identified traits and characteristics that generated negative perceptions about me. What shocked me was how completely blind I had been to many of the negative behaviors and character flaws that my focus group identified. It is difficult to describe the impact this report had on my self-esteem. It hurt. Essentially, in the span of a few minutes, the foundation on which I thought managing relationships rested had crumbled. The gap between how I believed people perceived me as a person and how they actually felt about me was so large, I felt there was no way to close it.

Fortunately, my coach was astute in helping business executives change, improve, and in some cases, reinvent themselves. She helped me see the changes I had to make. She convinced me that each person has a personal brand that has a profound impact on their success in business. Over the ensuing months, she helped me change the way I interacted with others. She taught me how to manage my interpersonal relationships in a way that improved the value of my brand. It was an excruciating process because I was required to put aside habits that had been ingrained through years of repetition. I had to learn new behaviors that were uncomfortable and awkward. In time, perceptions changed. Follow-up interviews with my focus group indicated that the way others viewed me (my brand) had made a dramatic improvement.

This painful and eye-opening process was a turning point for me. I was forced to acknowledge that my education, skills, talents, and accomplishments were not nearly as important as the quality of my interpersonal interactions. I learned that I had to stand in the shoes of my clients, prospects, peers, and employees. I had to view and understand myself through their eyes in order to maintain the integrity of my personal brand. I had to make regular adjustments to ensure it maintained its value. I learned that the real secret to success in business is getting people to buy you.

"A Brand Called You"

In a brilliant and often referenced article titled "A Brand Called You," management guru Tom Peters argued the case for personal branding: "Regardless of age, regardless of position, regardless of the business we happen to be in, all of us need to understand the importance of branding. We are CEOs of our own companies: Me Inc. To be in business today, our most important job is to be head marketer for the brand called You. It's that simple—and that hard. And that inescapable."

In his book, *Me 2.0,* personal branding guru, Dan Schwabel defines personal branding as ". . . the process by which individuals differentiate themselves and stand out from the crowd by identifying and articulating their unique value proposition, whether professional or personal, and then leveraging it across platforms with a consistent message and image to achieve a specific goal. In this way, individuals can enhance their recognition as experts in their field, establish reputation and credibility, advance their careers, and build self-confidence."

The simple definition of branding is the act of distinguishing one commodity, service, or product from another in order to create differentiation in the mind of the purchaser: Nike vs. adidas, Coke vs. Pepsi, Google vs. Yahoo!, Amazon vs. Barnes and Noble, Bayer Aspirin vs. Walgreen Aspirin.

Following this definition, personal branding is the act of distinguishing one's self from others in the same industry or field by creating differentiation in the mind of the customer, prospect, peer, or manager. As I learned through my experience and as Tom Peters articulates in his article, the concept is simple, but implementing it is not. It requires constant focus, self-discipline, and self-awareness. Your personal brand is the perception of others based on how they perceive you on the surface and their actual experience with you.

Your personal brand is a promise of the value customers, prospects, peers, employees, and managers will receive when investing their time with you. In her book, *Get Back to Work Faster,* bestselling author and sales guru, Jill Konrath, makes the case for this, writing that we each must have a value proposition that others perceive as tangible value to their business. Your personal brand is powerful when dealing with others because it replaces concerns about logical issues (price, terms and conditions, delivery times, quality, or experience) with the emotional decision to do business with you based on the belief that you, and only you, can truly solve their problems. This emotional connection to your brand will propel you to the upper echelons of your industry.

Building a Personal Brand

There is the misnomer that to build a personal brand you have to sell others on why you should be valued. You may recall this principle from earlier in the book, "People love to buy, but they hate to be sold." Building a strong personal brand is achieved primarily through actions. It is what you do versus what you say. Over time, this shapes the perceptions of those with whom you do business and most importantly generates *brand loyalty.* In every interaction with others, you are provided with an opportunity to differentiate yourself. This shapes and reinforces the perception that there is unique value in doing business with you. Everything you do and everything left undone, big and small, good or bad, is judged and the accumulated impact of those actions affects how others perceive the brand called You.

Action alone is not enough, though. Personal branding also requires you to invest in the ongoing process of managing your reputation and credibility. This enables those who have no direct experience with you to have a positive perception prior to actually meeting you, and those who have had an experience with you receive consistent messaging (positive emotional experiences) that reinforces their belief that you bring value as a problem solver. Not unlike branding a product or service, you must develop consistent messaging, positioning, and packaging that allow you to manage how others perceive you. In today's world, this means investing in both your online and offline presence.

This chapter is designed to provide you with the basic tools you need to build and manage the brand called You. As always, my goal is to keep things simple and easy to execute.

Interpersonal Relationships

As I explained in the opening story, the quality of your interpersonal relationships will always have the greatest impact on your personal brand. Imagine a real estate agent who spends thousands of dollars on advertising. He puts his face on billboards, on bus-stop benches, and in real estate magazines. He may build his brand awareness up to the point that his phone starts ringing; but, if he is an unlikable, self-centered jerk who is unable to connect, it will not take much time for his reputation to suffer. Word of mouth is far more powerful than billboards.

In the last five chapters, you discovered the five levers of *People Buy You*. These five levers are the most powerful tools you have in your branding toolbox. Be honest with yourself. Consider your relationships and recent interactions with other people. Think about it. How are you perceived?

Is Brand You Likable?

Are you consistently smiling, cheerful, and polite? How about manners? Do people perceive you as enthusiastic, optimistic, confident, and authentic?

Do You Connect?

Do people like being around you because you make them feel important? Do you take a genuine interest in others? Do you give others your complete attention and listen deeply? Do people feel that you listen to them?

Are You a Problem Solver?

Do you deliver value first by consistently focusing on and solving others' problems? Do you solve problems even if there is nothing in it for you? Are your customers loyal to you because you consistently solve their problems? Do people feel that you genuinely want to help them get what they want, not because it is in your best interest, but because it is in their best interest?

Are You Trustworthy?

Do you do what you say you will do? Can people count on you? Do you freely admit when you are wrong or have made mistakes, and do you apologize? Do others feel that you keep your promises?

Do You Create Positive Emotional Experiences?

Do you make the time and take the effort to make others feel good? Do you constantly think about how you can bring joy to the lives of your clients, prospects, managers, and peers? Do people look forward to seeing you? Do others feel anchored to you?

I realize that pondering this is difficult. If you and those who know you could answer yes, unequivocally,

to these questions, you would be unstoppable. However, the reality is that you are not perfect. You will
never be able to answer yes to all these questions all the
time. It is more important that you clearly understand
and internalize that, in each interaction with another
person, you have the opportunity to increase the value
of your personal brand or to hurt it. When you think
about it in this context, these questions will help you
self-correct when you find yourself in situations that
may damage your brand. That, by itself, will give you
a competitive edge few will match.

Manage Labels

Assigning labels to people and things is one of the
ways our brains make sense of the world around us.
With people, labels help us give meaning to intangi-
ble behaviors we observe. Labels can be good or bad.
Labels also stick and have the ability to influence others who may have had no direct observation of those
same behaviors. Mary is late for work a few days in a
row, and the boss labels her lazy. He tells other managers she is lazy in a staff meeting. A manager who
was considering promoting Mary into her department
is there, and decides it is no longer a good idea. Mary
was late not because she was lazy, but because her
4-year-old son had chicken pox and she had to find
someone to take care of him before she could come

to work. This label, right or wrong, accurate or not, has affected Mary's personal brand. Think this sounds absurd? Think again. It happens all of the time.

You label people and people label you. The words that people use to describe you impact how you are perceived. Are you aware of how people describe you? Do they say you are a hard worker, honest, intelligent? Do they label you smart, a good leader, loyal? Or, do people say you are lazy, arrogant, or talk too much? In some cases, no matter what you do, people will label you in a negative way. It is also unlikely that you will ever know all the labels people have given you. Protecting your brand means controlling the things that are in your control. This means managing the behaviors you allow others to observe. I've said this many times: in business, you are on stage. Every move you make is being watched and judged by others. It is up to you to develop the self-discipline to manage the behaviors that help you build your brand. For instance, if you want to be perceived as a team player, then volunteer for projects and extra work that benefits the team and the boss. If you want your brand to say "He has a commitment to excellence," go the extra mile in everything you do. If you want to be known as someone people can trust, then never make commitments you cannot keep, and deliver on promises.

Sometimes you will be given a negative label unfairly. If this happens, make every effort to speak with the person who is negatively labeling you directly. In a nonconfrontational manner, ask for the opportunity to change his or her opinion. This is best done with obvious humility in a neutral place like a coffee shop.

This tactic often works because you come across as an authentic human being, and most people are willing to give you a second chance. Sometimes you will let your guard down and behave in a way that is uncharacteristic of how you want to be perceived. When this happens, make a sincere apology. Then, do not let it happen again. If you have been consistent in your behavior, most people will forget a single slip. If you repeat the behavior, though, you may do irreparable harm to your brand.

Manage Your Professional Image

In addition to managing the interpersonal and behavioral perceptions others have of you, it is essential to control how they view you as a business professional. This includes obvious things like your physical appearance. How you dress, the kind of car you drive, the organization of your office, the clubs and organizations you belong to, your educational background, and the people you associate with all contribute to the perception. Since I did not intend for this book to delve into things like how to dress for business, I recommend that you buy and read current books on professional dress and etiquette. Even if you think you know it all, I believe you will find a review an eye opener.

Beyond outward appearance, the two most frequently overlooked opportunities to bolster professional image are positioning yourself as an expert and actively building to maintain a pristine online presence.

Become an Expert

One of the key characteristics of the most successful people is that they strive to become experts in their fields. When you become an expert in your company's products, services, and processes, other people in your organization will seek you out for help. This further strengthens your brand. When you become an expert in your industry, trade associations and industry groups will seek you out. When you become an expert in your field, you will be a better problem solver, and your clients will look to you as a consultant. In all cases, as an expert, you will be given opportunity after opportunity to help others get what they want (solve problems), which in turn will help you build a powerful personal brand.

Becoming an expert is much easier than you think. First, you have to study and absorb your subject matter. Second, you have to get others to present you as an expert to others.

Learn

Everything you need to know to be an expert in your field or industry, or your company's products or services has already been written, recorded, or is in a training manual. All you need is the commitment to learn. When you make the commitment to learn, a little bit every day, you will be shocked at how much you are able to absorb in a short period of time.

Read for 15 Minutes a Day

Top executives regularly consume more than 20 books a year. These super successful people clearly understand the power of reading books. So consider this: The average business book takes the average reader about three hours to complete. When you set aside just 15 minutes each day for professional reading, you will easily read more than 20 books each year. With e-Book readers like Amazon's Kindle and Barnes and Noble's nook, you have the ability to carry dozens of books with you in a light package, making it convenient to catch up on your professional reading at any time. Everything you ever need to know about anything is contained in a book. If you want to learn something or become an expert at something, all you have to do is read and study.

Take Advantage of Free Training

Most companies today offer copious amounts of free training. With the advent of learning management systems (LMS), a great deal of this training is available online and on demand. This free training is an incredible benefit because it gives you the opportunity to get out of the field and learn new concepts and practice new skills. Over the course of a year, these programs can add up to thousands of dollars in free training.

Stay Current in Your Field and Attend Seminars

To be seen as an expert in your industry, you must stay current. Subscribe to *and read* your industry's trade magazines, and go to industry events and seminars. There are experts on sales, business, and leadership who conduct seminars and who speak in virtually every city. Many people find it impossible to take time out of their busy schedules to attend these events. The truth is, you can't afford not to go. Some of the brightest minds in business are speaking in your city today. They are speaking to civic groups, chamber groups, or conducting stand-alone seminars.

Turn Your Radio Off

The average outside sales professional spends between 10 and 20 hours a week in a car. At a minimum, you have at least 30 minutes to an hour a day of commute time. Instead of wasting driving time listening to talk radio and music, listen to audio books and podcasts designed to improve your sales and business skills. The great Zig Ziglar calls this "Automobile University." Zig maintains that by just listening to audio programs in your car, you can gain the equivalent of a university education.

Leverage Technology

The sheer amount of free content available on the Internet for business professionals is unprecedented. Just a decade ago, you would have had to spend thousands of dollars to access a small portion of the information that can now be yours for free. With just the click of a mouse, you have immediate access to an incredible list of top experts and thought leaders. From Podcasts, to videos, to blogs, to e-zines, it is all at your fingertips.

Build Your Reputation as an Expert

How do experts become perceived as experts? They demonstrate that they are experts in their subject matter by writing, speaking, teaching, and coaching. Over time, as their bodies of work grow, so do their reputations as experts. It is important to understand that it is not about knowing the most or being the best. Instead, it is about having the courage to learn and then to demonstrate what you know in the service of others. When you volunteer to speak at sales meetings or other events, to lead trainings, to coach, and to write articles, you are building your body of work.

Teach and Coach

If you think about it, the people we admire the most and consider experts are teachers, trainers, and coaches. These individuals use what they have learned to help others gain a leg up. There are endless opportunities to teach and coach others in informal and structured environments. The best place to start is by volunteering to lead a training session at your next sales or staff meeting or to offer your services as a trainer in your company's training courses. Likewise, you can find opportunities to teach at trade-association events. If you become a technical subject-matter expert, it can lead to training opportunities at customer events. One of the very best ways to build your reputation as an expert is by volunteering to mentor new hires, college recruits, and less experienced people. These folks will not only feel loyalty to you for the help, they will tell others that you know your stuff.

Speak

Public speaking, besides being an excellent means of generating leads, is a powerful method for building your body of work as an expert. When you speak in public and do it well, the people in your audience instantly label you an expert. Speaking allows you to showcase your knowledge. It also gives you tremendous visibility and credibility. It creates the perception that you are an expert and authority in your field, and it creates an endless stream of qualified leads that come to you almost effortlessly. Because so few of your competitors do it, it will set you apart.

It is really easy to get speaking gigs. Start within your own company. Volunteer to speak at team meetings or training events. You will also find that organizations such as your industry's trade association, the chamber of commerce, rotary club, and other business and civic groups are always in need of guest speakers. All you really have to do is call and volunteer, and they will happily put you on the schedule. If you attend trade shows and association meetings, just call the meeting planners and tell them you would like to be speaker or put on a seminar. Meeting planners are always on the lookout for subject–matter experts to add value to their programs.

Write

Experts write. They write articles, blogs, and opinions. (People who make their living as experts write books.) Although writing a book may be a bit over the top for the average business professional, you should be writing articles and blogs regularly. Again, the opportunities abound. Virtually every written publication needs content. Begin with your company's newsletters. Call the editor and volunteer to write an article. Reach out to your industry trade organizations and volunteer to write for the association's trade publication, newsletter, or web site. They will welcome you.

Beyond a doubt, one of the very best ways to showcase your professional knowledge is with a blog. What makes a blog ideal is that you are in control. You are not at the mercy of editors, so you can write when, where, and what you want. Blogs ~ e easy and inexpensive to set up. WordPress, Typepad, and Blogger are all free or low cost options for bloggers.

What should you write about? Write about subjects that are relevant and timely to people in your industry and your customers' industries. Write about the things you know. Write about things you are passionate about. The more you write, the better you will get. In time, your body of work will expand, and others will cite and reference your articles. Your reputation as an expert will be cemented.

Manage Your Online Presence

Colin hung up the phone and just stood there, shaking his head. He had pulled strings to get his son, Perry, an

interview at one of the most well-respected account-
ing firms in the country. With an MBA from a top
tier business school and his connections, Perry should
have been a shoo-in. Then he got the call. Before
the offer letter went out, the hiring manager Googled
his son's name and found pictures of him doing bong
hits at a college party. These were pictures from five
years earlier that someone else had posted and tagged.
Nevertheless, Colin's son's personal brand had taken a
major hit and the offer was withdrawn—game over.

We live in the Age of Transparency. Anyone, any-
where, anytime can get a snapshot of you with a simple web search. Your managers, peers, prospects, and
people you meet *are* checking you out online. Savvy
prospects and customers are doing research on you
before meetings. What are they finding when they
Google you?

Your online presence plays a crucial role in building Brand You. If you ignore it, it will be at your own
peril. You must control what people find when they
search for you on the web. Yes, there are some things
you cannot control, as illustrated in Perry's case. You
have friends, family, and old college buddies who do
not consider the consequences when they post pictures of you doing stupid things. The beauty of search
engines, though, is that you can bury those harm-
ful images under the pages you want people to see.
All you really need to do is control the first two or
three pages on Google. There is very low probability

that anyone will search farther than page two. Recent studies have shown that fewer than eight percent of people go past the third page. But, what if you don't have an online presence? Over the years you've managed to avoid writing anything online, joining social networks, or having your name mentioned on anything by anyone. You are a blank slate. That's good, right? Wrong. When people are unable to find anything about you, the opportunity to build your personal brand is lost.

Managing Your Brand Online Is Not Difficult but It Does Take Vigilance

Set Up a Personal Web Site or Blog

Every professional should set up a personal web site, blog, or both. When possible, make your name (or a derivative of your name) the domain name. Include a bio, accomplishments, education, certificates, a professional photo and articles you have written. You may also wish to include links to other professional web sites and experts in your industry and/or learning resources you recommend. My suggestion is to go with a blog instead of a standalone web site. Blogs are easier to work with and more flexible. Whatever you choose, make sure it is professional and puts Brand You in the best light.

LinkedIn

I'll step out on a ledge and say that LinkedIn is the most important business networking tool in history. As a search engine for professionals, it is unparalleled. LinkedIn is one of the first places other professionals will look for you. It is a valuable tool with multiple uses for business professionals. For the purposes of building Brand You, focus on your profile page. If you do not have an account on LinkedIn, I recommend you get one now. Once you have your account set up, build your profile. It should include a short bio, your work history, education, and your photo. Ensure that your profile reflects the professional image you wish to portray. Be sure to indicate that you want your profile to be visible to search engines. This way, when people use search engines to find information on you, your LinkedIn profile will be among the first things they find.

Social Networking

Other social networking sites like Facebook, SalesGravy.com, Plaxo, and Twitter provide you with the opportunity to set up a professional profile that can easily be found via online search. The same process applies. Ensure your new profiles and existing profiles are professional and reflective of the brand you wish to build.

Article Marketing

Because writing is foundational to being perceived as an expert, you will want to publish your articles online. Once published, your articles will also be the first items found when people search for you online. Where should you publish? Look for industry blogs that accept guest bloggers, your trade association web site, and content aggregators that allow you to create a professional profile and post articles. There are several hundred article sites on the Internet that accept articles. These sites are always hungry for new content. Many are niche sites like SalesGravy.com that are built around a particular business subject, whereas others like eZineArticles.com are general sites that accept a wide range of articles.

Google Alerts

Google has a wonderful tool called *Google Alerts* designed for monitoring what people are saying about you online. It is free and easy to set up. Go to http://www.google.com/alerts.

In managing your online presence, you won't build Rome in a day. It will take months and even years to build a body of work online. It is absolutely vital that you start. Don't let the prospect overwhelm you. Do a little bit every day, and over time, your online presence will become a cornerstone of Brand You.

Attack Yourself

Eventually the hard work and effort you have placed into honing your *People Buy You* skills and building Brand You will pay off. Your accomplishments will pile up. Your professional network will grow. You will receive promotions, close big deals, and win awards. You will go on president's club trips. You will be recognized and respected as an expert. Your customers will love you. You will prosper. Nothing feels better than winning. But while you are cashing that big bonus check, relaxing on the beach, or walking on stage at your national sales meeting to pick up your big trophy, ask yourself this question: "What is next?"

Getting there was hard. It required perseverance, training, hard work, and focus. But it is human nature, after we start winning, to take our foot off the success accelerator and just coast for awhile. To relax too long in the glow of victory and false confidence lets our guard down and we forget that the game is still on. We allow old habits to reemerge. Do not leave the door open to failure.

I once saw a magazine advertisement from a company that was touting an award it had just received. The ad simply read:

"When you're in second place, attack the leader. When you're in first place, Attack Yourself."

What a perfect message! In the twenty-first century there is no time for complacency. You cannot afford the luxury of letting up for even a moment. There is no time to rest easy. Learn to take each win in stride and raise your own bar so you keep reaching higher. It is easy to look back at poor performance or a failure with 20/20 vision and find all the areas where improvement can be made. It takes loads of self-discipline and the heart of a winner to break down a brilliant performance and then take action to make small adjustments and improvements that keep you ahead of the pack. The great NFL quarterback, Steve Young, said once that "the principle is competing against yourself. It's about self-improvement, about being better than the day before."

Real winners constantly attack themselves. They pick apart each performance and seek ways to improve. It is the unwavering focus on constant improvement that separates the good from the great. Never forget that, in business, the most powerful weapon in your arsenal is *you*. It requires constant vigilance to remain likable, to connect, to solve problems, to remain trustworthy, and to create positive emotional experiences for others. People do not buy words, marketing campaigns, advertisements, sales pitches, products, services, or slick presentations. **People Buy You.**